Dad swathing, 1971

 FriesenPress

Suite 300 - 990 Fort St
Victoria, BC, V8V 3K2
Canada

www.friesenpress.com

ISBN
978-1-5255-3599-4 (Hardcover)
978-1-5255-3600-7 (Paperback)
978-1-5255-3601-4 (eBook)

1. BIOGRAPHY & AUTOBIOGRAPHY, PERSONAL MEMOIRS

Distributed to the trade by The Ingram Book Company

FIELDS AND FENCELINES

STORIES OF LIFE ON A FAMILY FARM

MARK E. HILLENBRAND

For Dad, whose example continues to guide me

Feeding the chickens, August 1981

CHAPTER 1
BEST DAY EVER

I love the musty smell of freshly tilled soil, and the way it cushions the feet and wraps around naked toes. As a child, I would walk barefoot behind the tractor as my dad tilled the land, watching for worms, mysterious rocks, and any other treasures that the process might reveal. Even as a youngster too small to help, I was left to believe my presence added value, so I grew up on the heels of my father and found my identity in the land long before anything else could take root. I was not simply raised on a farm, I was born to it.

1

I cannot recall a time in my life when I did not actively and willingly participate in the daily activities of the farm. My dad often boasted that he "started working at two years of age and hasn't quit since." While I cannot, with a clear conscience, make the same claim, I do know that I was "choring" by the age of four. I gathered eggs, fed chickens, cleaned barns, and tended to the rabbits with enthusiasm and dedication. For me, working on the farm was about being needed, spending time with the family, and making a tangible difference each and every day. I would sit back at the end of the day and enjoy the ache in my muscles while I reflected on all that I had accomplished.

I remember the day I finally gathered the courage to ask Dad if I could help with seeding during the upcoming spring. At best I was ten years old, but already I desperately wanted to be behind the wheel of a tractor in the fields. I rehearsed the conversation in my head for weeks beforehand. I would present a strong and logical case. I knew every field like the back of my hand, I would promise to stay far from fences and power poles, and I would watch the warning gauges incessantly, stopping the tractor at even the slightest hint of trouble. After all, it made no sense for the family to hire a man to help when I was willing, ready, and in my mind, more than able to do the job.

Scared of rejection, I waited patiently for the perfect opportunity. It would be some evening when the weather was particularly nice and Mom had exceeded all expectations with supper. After the meal, but before dessert, I would crack a few jokes at the expense of my sisters to lighten the mood and then pop the question. When the moment finally arrived, my heart was pounding a mile a minute; it was now or never.

"Dad," I blurted, "I was thinking maybe I could drive the tractor this spring. I mean, there's too much work for you and I could harrow and stuff with the little tractor. Only in the fields with no power poles. You could even do the first round and ride around with me for a bit if you wanted."

The table grew silent as my family sat shocked at my attempt to thrust myself into manhood. Dad cracked a smile as he contemplated my request.

"Well, Mark, we'll see. You might not be quite ready for that yet."

Disappointed, I slumped deep into my chair and resolved to work harder. I was ready; he would see.

Then one day later that summer it happened. I was sitting outside on the lawn with my sisters after lunch on a hot summer day in July. My boots were off and I was wriggling my toes in the cool grass as Dad came out of the house. Doing a poor job of hiding his own excitement, he said abruptly, "Put your boots on, Mark. I think I'm going to get you to do a little harrowing."

My jaw dropped as I frantically scrambled to get my socks and boots back on before Dad could change his mind. My sisters giggled as I ran to catch up to Dad, who was already halfway down the yard.

I caught up with Dad as he was climbing aboard the red, open-air Massey Ferguson tractor. The diesel engine roared to life as Dad turned the key and together we drove over to an old rusty set of shaker harrows, which had sat abandoned in the far corner of the yard for many years. I guided him as he backed the tractor toward the archaic implement and helped hitch the harrows to the drawbar. We rode up to the shop and forced grease into the bearings to ensure the outdated machine was up to the task. While Dad slowly circled the implement, carefully checking each bolt and chain, I repeatedly commented on what good shape the old harrows were in, concerned that Dad would find a mechanical flaw and I would not be able to proceed. The harrows met with Dad's approval so we pulled into the field beside the house with the harrows squeaking and scratching behind us. Once around with Dad driving, explaining not to

3

oversteer, watch for rocks, and do not let the harrows plug with straw. Then Dad stopped the tractor, flashed a quick smile, and told me to take over.

I slid into the seat, gripped the steering wheel with fists white with excitement, put that little tractor in gear, and proceeded to harrow that field to the best of my ability. The smell of diesel in the air, the roar of the engine filling my ears, the wind and sun biting at my face, I loved it all. Round and round I went for the rest of the afternoon, waving at motorists as I circled past the road while the harrows broke up the stubble behind me. People honked when they saw me and grinned at the sight of a smiling, skinny little farm kid dragging an old rusty pair of harrows around a summer-fallow field. I felt so grown up that day, so important and needed as I scratched the soil, never tiring, never bored. I know now that that field did not need to be worked, and those old harrows have never been used since, but of all the accomplishments I have had in my life, few have been more memorable than that day.

I have spent most of my adult life chasing the emotions of that day. That deep, fulfilling sense of satisfaction that comes from doing the work you were meant for. I have found it in bits and pieces through the years, but it was always fleeting. Nothing has come close to the years I spent working the land beside my father.

That, perhaps, is why I am so thankful for having grown up on a family farm. There was never a period in my youth when I did not feel important and needed. I awoke each day with a set of expectations. Certain tasks had to be completed and it was my responsibility to see to it that they were done correctly. I took great pride in my work, striving to impress my parents in hopes of earning the right to assume additional responsibilities. I honestly cannot remember a single time in my life when I once complained or went about my chores upset, thinking about the other activities I could be devoting my time to. As far as I was concerned, there was simply nothing better to be doing than farming.

Grandma Hillenbrand, Mom, Aunt Elsbeth, Aunt Ruth,
and Dad, shucking peas, 1967

CHAPTER 2
GRANDPA'S JOURNEY

Lured by the promise of a better life and fascinated by stories
he had read in books and pamphlets, my paternal grandfather,
Leonhard Hillenbrand, left his native Germany in 1928 and
began the long trek to Canada.

Settling in Gravelbourg, Saskatchewan, Grandfather began

working as a farmhand, accepting work from anyone who was willing to hire a German-speaking immigrant ten years after the end of the Great War. Fortunately, Grandfather's experience farming in Germany, combined with a certificate in agriculture from a German technical school, made work easier to find than it may have been otherwise, and within a relatively short period he had managed to save enough money to purchase a farm of his own. In 1929, at the age of thirty, he packed his belongings and headed north to the Brightholme district of Saskatchewan, where he purchased a quarter section of farmland.

The original quarter of land came complete with a small, two-storey house boasting two small bedrooms upstairs, another on the main floor, a tiny kitchen, and a modest living room. A small woodstove was left with the onerous responsibility of heating the entire house, a task that it had a great deal of trouble accomplishing on cold winter nights.

There was no electricity, no running water, and no plumbing. Light and heat were supplied by lanterns and the woodstove. If water was required, Grandpa walked to the well with bucket in hand; lowered the bucket into the deep, dark hole; and hoped that when the pail was retrieved it would be full of water.

The house sat upon a rise one mile directly west of the mighty North Saskatchewan River. Rolling hills scattered with stunted poplars, willows, and shrubs, and sprinkled with patches of wild raspberries, chokecherries, and saskatoons covered both sides of the river valley. West of the river, the rugged valley gave way to gentle, undulating knolls blanketed with tall, lush poplars evidencing the rich, black soil that lay beneath. My grandfather carved fields from the forest, making room for oats, barley, and wheat. Barns were constructed from the timber and were quickly filled with chickens, cattle, horses, and pigs.

Two miles to the south of the farmyard sat the Church of God where Grandpa was able to worship in his native tongue each

Sunday alongside other German immigrants. Twelve and a half miles to the north lay the tiny town of Shellbrook, where clothing, tools, and other necessities could be purchased. Travelling to town for supplies was a major undertaking. Grandpa would rise at the break of dawn, hurry outside to milk the cows and tend to the animals, hitch the horses to the wagon, make the three-hour journey into town on the dusty trail, purchase the necessary goods, and ride three hours back home only to be greeted by a yard full of hungry animals that required his attention before he could retire for the evening. It was a lonely life of solitude and hard work, which is perhaps why Grandfather made the long trek back to Germany in December of 1934 in search of a bride.

After weeks of travel by train and then ship, Grandfather arrived back in the village of his birth, Sechselbach. Exhilarated by the sights and sounds of home, Grandfather soon began to mingle about the small town, visiting the family and friends he had left behind six years earlier. Among his stops was the schoolhouse, where a young man by the name of Leonhard Wolfmeyer, an acquaintance of Grandpa's, had been assigned the trying task of educating the local children from grades one through eight.

To Grandfather's surprise, Leonhard was enjoying the company of an attractive young lady, his sister Emma, who was visiting from nearby Blaufelden. As the three began to talk, Grandpa soon became less interested in Leonhard and more interested in Emma. In the days and weeks that followed, the young couple was seen together more and more frequently, talking and sharing the stories of their lives.

On April 4, 1935, Emma Wolfmeyer and Leonhard Hillenbrand, accompanied by their wedding party, walked hand in hand down the cobblestone streets of Blaufelden. The traditional German marriage parade took them from the

Wolfmeyer's family home to the local Lutheran church while family and friends lined the streets to cheer and shout their congratulations. The church was decorated with ribbons and evergreen boughs and the couple made their way up the tall, sweeping steps and into the quaint church constructed of stone and timber some four hundred years earlier. There, on that cool spring day, in front of family, friends, and God, the couple exchanged vows and were married.

Not surprisingly, Grandma's family was less than excited at the prospect of young Emma heading off across the ocean to live in a foreign land with a man she had known for less than five months. Grandma would chuckle when retelling the story of their engagement and how her brothers hastily took Grandfather aside to "enquire" as to his intentions and make it abundantly clear that their sister best be treated with the love and respect she deserved. Like her brothers, Grandma was apprehensive about her decision and the accompanying move. She would be leaving behind her parents, two sisters, four brothers, cousins, aunts, uncles, friends, and the only life she had ever known in exchange for a small shack in a rugged land where she would not even be able to speak the language. In Germany she had electricity and running water. In Germany Grandma had never in her life walked to a well for water or lit a kerosene lamp for light. In Germany the store, the school, the church, the library, the train, and every other modern convenience of the time were mere minutes from her door.

Two weeks after the wedding, as her family and friends waved goodbye with damp eyes and heavy hearts, Grandma boarded the train with her new husband and began the long trek to Canada. The couple travelled from Blaufelden to Luxembourg City and from Luxembourg City to the port city of Bremerhoffen, where they, along with hundreds of other Germans, boarded the *Stuttgart* bound for Canada. Lowered

9

into the hold were crates packed with all of Grandma's worldly possessions. Suitcases full of clothes and wedding gifts, chairs, several wooden and wicker chests, dressers, a beautiful hand-crafted mirror and table, a linen closet, a sewing machine, Grandpa's accordion, and even an organ.

For most of the nine-day crossing, Grandma lay huddled in their small cabin, violently ill as the ocean tossed the ship. Unable to eat or drink, Grandma lay wondering if she would live to see her new home. At one point in the journey, when she was actually feeling well enough to stand, Grandma stumbled out of the cabin and attempted to make her way to the dining hall for some food when the ship's captain happened upon her and exclaimed with a laugh, "My, I see even the half-dead ones are up and about today!"

After what seemed like an eternity, the ocean gave way to land, and the ship docked in Halifax, Nova Scotia, Canada. While excited to leave the misery of the ship behind her, Grandma's journey was far from over. From Halifax, the new-lyweds travelled by train for three days and nights, arriving in Winnipeg, Manitoba, on the morning of the fourth day. Once in Winnipeg, Grandpa hurried around the city buying supplies while his bewildered and weary bride followed hastily behind him, marvelling at the strange architecture, the dusty streets, and the gibberish spewing from the mouths of strangers.

That evening they boarded another train and travelled through the night, arriving in Shellbrook, Saskatchewan, the next morning, May 1, 1935. As Grandma stepped from the pas-senger car, her foot promptly sank into a foot of snow, which had been dumped by a spring storm. An ironically appropriate welcome for the exhausted and frightened newcomer. With snow spilling into her shoes and the wind biting at her naked face, Grandma trudged through the frozen terrain and followed Grandpa into a waiting automobile owned by Richard Schmaltz, a local farmer. Richard was a friend of Grandpa's and a fellow German immigrant, who had graciously agreed to meet the bride and groom upon their arrival. Grandma sat shivering in the car while Richard and Grandpa began the task of retrieving the possessions brought from Germany. Once the car had been filled to capacity, the trio made their way to the Schmaltz residence where they were welcomed into a warm house and given food. It must have been very comforting for Grandma to walk into the Schmaltz house that first night after her long, hard journey and be greeted by fellow Germans. Not simply because it was an opportunity to make new friends and rest after a gruelling two weeks of travel, but also because the Schmaltzes had made the same journey years earlier. They too had left family and friends behind and had managed to make a good and satisfying life for themselves in Canada. They had made new friends, had children, and had found their place in this foreign land. The Schmaltzes represented hope and promise for her new life.

Following breakfast the next morning, Grandma once again climbed into the car to begin the final leg of her journey. Sitting quietly in the back of the vehicle, Grandma's heart pounded as the car rumbled toward her new home. At each bend, her stomach swelled and her breathing halted as she politely stretched her small frame forward and strained her eyes, both hoping and dreading to catch a glimpse of her new home. Would it be as Leonhard had described? Would she be welcomed? Would she be happy? Suddenly the car began to slow. Leonhard turned toward Emma and with a mischievous smile softly whispered, "We're here."

Grandpa stepped from the car and stood tall with pride, deeply breathing in the air while his eyes scanned the yard, searching for anything that may be out of place. With everything as he had left it, he quickly spun on his heel, flung open the back door of the car, and smiling ear to ear, offered his hand to

Emma, still sitting quietly inside the vehicle, taking stock of her situation. With a gentle smile, her eyes met her husband's. She took his extended hand and carefully exited the car. Together they stood, hand in hand, while Emma absorbed the sights and sounds of the new world, and the new life, that lay before her. For the first time, she saw the small pale house where five of her six children would be born, the barns where she would milk cows and tend to horses, the well that she would now be walking to for water, and the fields where she would plant and harvest beside her husband. Even more pronounced, perhaps, were the things that Emma could not see. The local store, the beautifully manicured parks of Blaufelden, her church, her sisters, brothers, and friends that no longer surrounded her and would not comfort her again until her return to Germany twenty-eight years later.

My grandmother was not one to complain. She was almost always stoic, tough, and determined. I am quite sure that, on that cool spring day in 1935, she was no different. At the age of twenty-five, Emma had, in a very real sense, been born again. In her own words, it was "night and day" from all she was accustomed to. Apparently, it was a rather significant adjustment for the cattle as well, for, as Grandma approached, they began to stampede and snort their disapproval at the sight of a woman, a creature they had not previously experienced.

Grandma made her peace with the cows and all the barnyard creatures and was soon a competent, hardworking farm wife. Tending a garden, mending clothes, cooking, cleaning, washing, and caring for the chickens, cattle, horses, and pigs all became part of her regular daily routine. For years at a time, Grandma did not leave the boundaries of the farm. She would faithfully stay at home to tend to the chores when Grandpa went to town for supplies. She never attended a dance, a play, or a movie. There were no elaborate holidays, no weekends at the beach.

It was a simple, solitary existence. Outside of the occasional visit from neighbours, or a musical selection provided by my grandfather on his accordion, organ, or a carefully selected poplar leaf, their entire social calendar centred around the church, which is perhaps why my grandmother was a woman of unshakeable faith. Her faith gave her comfort and strength in all that she did. The church provided a refuge from the daily toil. It was a chance to meet and laugh with friends. An opportunity to draw from the strength and support of those around her.

In 1937, Emma gave birth to a daughter, Ingeborg. Two sons soon followed: Kurt, my father, in 1938 and Manfred in 1939. Just as life was beginning to assume a comfortable familiarity in Canada, it was being torn apart in Germany. Adolph Hitler was beginning to aggressively pursue his vision of obtaining "breathing room" for a united German people, and the mighty German war machine was on the move. Assuming a portion of the collective German guilt for the atrocities inflicted upon the world by her compatriots under Hitler's reign, Grandma always preferred to avoid the subject of war and Hitler. "Oh children," she would exclaim, frowning and shaking her head. "It is so hard to understand; you had to be there to see. It all started so good."

Hitler promised food for every pot. Work and stability in a strong, rejuvenated country. He promised to bring pride and dignity back to a country that had been ravaged by the First World War and humiliated by the treaty that finally brought peace. Who would not vote for such things? Who would not be excited to have such a leader? My great-grandfather Hillenbrand was a man who my grandmother deeply respected and admired. "Grandpa Hillenbrand, he was a very wise man, and, oh," Grandma would announce with conviction, shaking her fist for emphasis, "he thought Hitler was such a good man. Now the country would be strong, people would have jobs, and food and good lives." But then, slowly, it started to change. Little by little, so it was not even noticeable at first. Suddenly, mysteri-ously, everyone was wearing a swastika on their lapel, houses were decorated with flags and banners, and propaganda began popping up around town. Children were encouraged to join the Hitler Youth where they would be taught the value of friend-ship, hard work, and, of course, white supremacy and German expansion, while women were asked to attend Party rallies on Sundays, which took them away from church and slowly replaced traditional religion with Socialist philosophies. Those that weren't Party supporters began to have trouble finding work, and life was becoming increasingly difficult for Jews, Gypsies, and other minorities. By the time my grandmother left Germany in 1935, my great-grandfather, along with many other Germans, was questioning the wisdom of Hitler, but by that time Germany was on a path of no return.

In 1938, Carl Wolfmeyer, my grandmother's oldest brother, was conscripted into the German army and left for war. Two more brothers, Albert and Georg, soon followed, leaving only Leonhard, a teacher, behind, exempt from service to ensure a new generation of German soldiers would learn to read and write. Communication with Germany became almost impos-sible during the war. For a time, Grandma was able to pass com-munications through an American soldier, but for the last years of the war, there was no way to tell how the family was manag-ing. Imagine how difficult that must have been. Thousands of miles from home, trying to raise a young family in a country where the neighbours have been sent across the ocean to fight her brothers and destroy her homeland. I am sure my grand-parents must have suffered prejudice at the hands of others and struggled personally as they tried to make sense of their divided loyalties.

As with all things in life, the war came to an end. Europe slowly began the painstaking task of rebuilding decimated cities and burying its dead. As the world began to heal, the lines of communication were reopened and Grandma received a letter from her family in Germany. Shaking with dread at the possibility of what its contents may reveal, Grandma tore open the envelope and began to read: "Dear Emma, we are so thankful this dreadful war has finally ended. We pray that all is well for you and Leonhard in Canada and we are all so grateful that you were spared the agony of these last terrible years." As she continued to read, she discovered, to her joy, that bombs had not fallen on Blaufelden and that her lovely town was very much as she had left it. Her sisters and parents were well and were all struggling to rebuild their country and their lives. And then, almost as an afterthought in hopes that the news would be easier to bear, the letter announced that Georg had not returned home. He had been classified as missing in action in 1944 and was presumed to have died (a reality that was confirmed many years later by a fellow soldier who claimed to have seen his corpse on the side of the road as the German army was making a hasty retreat). Shaking with grief, Grandma reached for a pencil and paper and replied. Weeping as she wrote, Grandma explained that all was well in Canada and that they had managed quite well during the war. She expressed her gratitude that the war had spared her home and, of course, expressed her deep sadness that the war had claimed the life of her brother Georg. "But what of Albert, Carl, and Leonhard?" she asked. "How are they and their families?"

Several weeks later, another letter arrived. Grandma hurriedly opened it, expecting that all the bad news had been shared. It hadn't. "Dearest Emma, with great sadness we write to tell you that your brother Albert died in battle on the Russian front in June of 1942." Fearful that the news of two deaths would be too difficult to bear at one time, Albert's fate had purposely been left out of the first letter. As the tears began to roll down her cheeks once again, Grandma continued to read, "Amidst our grief we give thanks for Carl as he has returned home. He was seriously wounded and the bitter Russian cold has claimed all the toes on his right foot, but he is alive and well among us."

Numb with grief, Grandma once again reached for pencil and paper and wearily began to scrawl a reply in which she expressed her sorrow and asked, as before, how Leonhard was managing, was his family well, had his school been spared? As if anticipating the question, a third letter soon arrived and regretfully revealed the final secret.

In the spring of 1945, the German army was all but defeated. Allied troops were rapidly liberating European towns and cities and were pushing toward Germany with seemingly unstoppable momentum. Germany would fall and Hitler's dream had long since become a nightmare. In these final days of the war, Leonhard was teaching in Brettheim, a German town located in the German interior. As the war ravaged around him, and as pupils and resources dwindled, Leonhard continued to work, doing his best to ensure that the children of Germany were equipped for a future without war. His diligence and perseverance had not gone unnoticed. Leonhard had been elevated to the position of Ortsgruppenleiter (head of the local Nazi party) and was an admired and respected man in the community.

In early April of 1945, the American army was a mere seven kilometres from Brettheim and was determined to continue pushing northward toward Berlin. Brettheim lay directly in its path. The result was inevitable; Brettheim would fall. It was simply a matter of when, not if.

Foolish and frightened, the Hitler Youth began to organize, determined to raise a final offensive for the glory of the Führer. Four young boys, blinded by patriotism and arrogance, gathered weapons and prepared to drive the Americans back. As they began their march toward the enemy, they were confronted by several townspeople who demanded they put their weapons down and abandon their foolishness lest the town, and more lives, be needlessly lost. There was simply no need for more suffering, enough blood had already been spilled, and a handful of poorly armed boys could not change the course of the war. The men wrestled the guns from the hands of the youth. Scolding them for their foolishness, they sent them all home before proceeding to dispose of their weapons in the local lake.

Not all of the boys returned home, however. Humiliated by their reprimand, a disgruntled few ran to the ranks of the notorious S.S. and reported the incident. Unable to tolerate acts of such gross insubordination, even in the last days of the war, the S.S. hastily interrogated residents, seeking to discover who among them had quashed the resistance. A local farmer, Freidrich Hanselmann, a grandfather to two of the youth, was singled out and condemned to death for his role in the disarmament. Being the local Nazi party leader, Leonhard, along with the mayor, Leonhard Gackstatter, was directed to sign the death sentence. They both refused to do so. They would play no part in such injustice. It was a deliberate and courageous decision, but it sealed their fate, for they too were then condemned to death.

On April 10, 1945, the three men were delivered to the town's cemetery where wooden chairs had been placed beneath a sturdy linden tree and a noose for each fashioned from rough twine. With callous familiarity, the ropes were thrown around extended branches and fastened securely. A solider then thrust out his arm and began to push Leonhard toward his waiting gallows. Disgusted at the actions of his countrymen, Leonhard broke free from the soldier's grasp and glared at him with contempt, dumbfounded and repulsed by the insanity that surrounded him. In a final display of courage, Leonhard walked unaccompanied toward the chair and stepped up onto it. He reached upward, fitted the noose snugly around his own neck, and rocked the chair forward, leaving behind a pregnant wife, four children, and the American army only a few hours' march away. He was thirty-six years old.

Friedrich Hanselmann, Leonhard Gackstatter, and Leonhard Wolfmeyer

On April 17, 1945, the American army advanced. The S.S. had ordered the infantry to defend the town at all costs, so for eight hours, artillery, tanks, and attack bombers relentlessly pounded the village, reducing it to a burning inferno before it fell.

Grandma carried the scars of loss her entire life and was well into her nineties before, after gentle prodding, she finally shared with me the story of Leonhard's passing. I recall sitting in her small kitchen, drinking tea, and watching her eyes dampen with tears as she relived the memories. She spoke not only of her devastation upon learning the news initially, but also of the heartache that followed her for the rest of her life.

"There were nights," she said, "when I was milking cows alone in the barn and an image of Leonhard would suddenly fill my mind." Grandma paused, the hurt still visible. "And I would have to stand up and pace against the glow of the lantern, lest my grief pull me to the earth."

It is hard to comprehend what it must have been like to carry that pain. My grandma stood tall and took the weight; she never allowed her sorrow to suppress her smile. Despite a life marked with sacrifice and loss, she remained eternally grateful for what she had and paid little mind to what she did not. You will find what you look for in life; my grandma chose to look for blessings, and she found them in abundance.

Erin, Heather, Grandma Hillenbrand, Aunt Iris, Aunt Inga, Colleen, me, Dad, and Mom celebrating Grandma Hillenbrand's birthday, 1983

Hillenbrand Farm, 1986

CHAPTER 3
THE LAND

Our Shellbrook, Saskatchewan, farm was located in the northern region of the province's grain belt. If you were to hop in your car and head straight north of Shellbrook for a leisurely Sunday drive, you would only need to travel approximately forty kilometres before noticing that the number of fields and frequency of farmyards was decreasing. By the time the odometer reached sixty kilometres, you would find yourself surrounded by the lush virgin forests and the plentiful lakes and streams of Prince Albert National Park. We never had to travel far to find the lake, river, golf course, or secluded berry patch of our choice.

Unlike our southern counterparts, who simply took a plow to open prairie on every acre that is now cropped, our farm was originally blanketed in dense forest. When my grandfather purchased the original section of land, only a small portion of that 640 acres was cleared. So Grandfather diligently continued breaking the land to make way for cattle barns, grain bins, and wheat fields. When my dad succeeded Grandfather, he continued the process, each year expanding arable acres in a quest to increase overall production and achieve a financially viable operation.

Whenever my father would tell stories of breaking the land, I always felt as if I had missed a great adventure. Men and machinery toiling away, clearing away the forest to reveal the rich, dark soil together with the history of the land. I remember the awe I felt as a child when my dad would display Aboriginal artifacts that he had discovered while clearing the land of the trees. Carefully wrapped in a blue cloth and tied securely with a piece of string were spearheads, arrowheads, hammerheads, and even bags of pemmican still preserved within their original leather sacks. I would hold these items in my hands and marvel at the thought of a people inhabiting the land long before my grandfather boarded that ship from Germany. To think that at one time indigenous peoples hunted and fished in the very valleys and lakes that surround our farm; that they camped less than a kilometre from where our house stood, cooked berries and buffalo together, and then buried it deep within the ground only for it to be uncovered by my father many years later was fascinating to me.

Of the 960 acres that ultimately made up our family farm,

perhaps 200 remain sheltered in the same natural ecosystem that has flourished since the beginning of time. Fields carved out of the forest are sheltered from ravaging winds that would otherwise sweep unchecked across the land, and the cattle have a cool refuge from the blistering sun on a hot July afternoon. Leaving the trees also meant that we could continue to selectively log the timber that has given us barns, machinery sheds, grain bins, and a home.

Aside from the economic and environmental advantages, leaving the remaining forest intact was ultimately about maintaining a natural balance. The trees, shrubs, and ecosystem they support have an intrinsic value separate and distinct from any monetary figure. If the forest continues, so do family picnics, wildlife, and the annual Christmas tree search.

As children, my sisters and I would often head into the woods for camping adventures. On one occasion, as a six-year-old, I planned a particularly challenging excursion. For weeks beforehand, I read any wilderness book I could get my hands on in preparation for the journey that lay ahead, and convinced that being stranded over winter was a real possibility (and secretly hoping it would happen), I left nothing to chance. I learned about the wild animals of the region, which plants could be used for food, and which held medicinal properties. I read how to construct makeshift splints and field dressings, how to snare rabbits, build fires, and generally survive for extended periods of time in our cattle pasture.

Once satisfied that I had sufficiently educated myself regarding the art of wilderness survival, the next step was to recruit a team of brave fellow adventurers. My sister Heather immediately came to mind. While not a particularly gifted outdoorsperson, she did possess exceptional strength for a seven-yearold and could help pack gear. Besides, with a united front, Mom was less likely to veto the adventure. With Heather on board, our neighbour Robbie was contacted. Robbie assured me he too was up to the challenge. My scheme was coming to fruition.

The plan was simple. We would meet at our house the night before to review the maps I had painstakingly drawn with pencil crayons on second-hand paper and discuss the dangers that lay ahead. A briefing was critical in order that I might ensure each member of the team possessed the necessary mental sharpness and physical toughness to withstand the rigours awaiting them. Following the meeting, we all retired to bed early in our playhouse loft, excited to wake at the crack of dawn to begin our trek.

At first light, I rustled the troops into action. A lunch was quickly packed as I double-checked the gear: wilderness books, Band-Aids, water, matches, a pocketknife, a blanket in case we were overcome with exhaustion and needed to nap, and of course, my trusty air rifle with plenty of extra ammo.

I assured my parents that the journey would be long and hard and not to expect us back for supper; in fact, it would only be by the grace of God if we were to make it back at all. With a quick goodbye, the three of us were off toward the cattle pasture and the deepest, darkest part of the woods.

About ten minutes into our journey, and about twenty minutes after breakfast, my companions began to complain that they were hungry and that we should stop for lunch. I was beginning to question the wisdom of my choices and contemplated sending the weak home so as not to be distracted from my goal. Twenty minutes later, believing that we had been hiking for several hours, I relented and agreed to sit down for a well-deserved break.

Following our meal, and after a quick lesson from me on what to do if we encountered hostile wildlife, we resumed our adventure. On and on we trudged as fast as our little legs could carry us, over big rotting logs and under drooping branches.

After what seemed like hours, the dark forest gave way and we saw the familiar sight of home. We had made it! Our journey had taken us on a full circle through the pasture and deposited us back at the far end of the yard where Dad was busy feeding the cattle. Excited that our exploration had been a success and believing that we had been gone all day, I ran toward Dad, shouting and waving my arms. Upon seeing this display Dad become concerned that some misfortune had fallen upon us and ran to meet me.

"What's wrong?" he asked, searching my face for signs of distress and unconsciously counting my fingers and limbs.

"Nothing. We are back from our hike," I announced triumphantly. Grinning from ear to ear at our marvellous accomplishment, I asked, "Did we make it back in time for supper?"

"Mark," Dad replied with a smile, "you made it back in time for more breakfast if you want; you've been gone less than an hour."

This news was a great disappointment to me. An hour hike was hardly worth bragging about to my friends. Deflated, I trudged sheepishly up to the house and unpacked all our gear before trotting back out into the yard to help Dad with the chores.

The events of that day must have permanently scarred Heather because she refused to accompany me on any further adventures. Fortunately, I was blessed with two other younger, more impressionable sisters who filled in nicely in Heather's absence.

At least once per summer, I would enthusiastically announce to Colleen (one year younger than I) and Erin (five years younger) that a camping trip had been planned and that they were fortunate enough to have been selected to accompany me on the journey. Such invitations had to be handled very delicately. While Colleen and Erin were certainly not all ribbons and lace, they would have been just as happy to spend the night in the comfort of their beds. If I was to convince them to spend the better part of a day away from their Barbie dolls, crammed into a small pup tent, some slick salesmanship was going to be necessary.

I would remind them that the fresh air and exercise would do them good, that camping was an adult activity, and (my personal favourite and a very effective weapon over the years) that the sisters of my friends always accompanied their brothers on such excursions and that their failure to do so would certainly not be looked upon favourably by the community.

If only I had a brother! We could have spent nights whispering under blankets of the certain death and wild adventure that awaited us. How the likelihood of seeing a bear was a real possibility and that we would almost certainly encounter savage coyotes. But alas, we must play the cards we are dealt. So I spoke of a gentle hike among pleasant trails to a meadow full of flowers when in truth I wanted to arm each of us with knives and air rifles and march into the thickest part of the forest where in my imagination we would discover that we were a refugee family fleeing the horror of some great war, forced to scratch out an existence in the wilds of the Northern Parkland. Fortunately, Colleen was the agreeable sort and Erin was so much younger that she would have probably filled her pockets with cow dung if it allowed her to be included with her older siblings.

With the troops on board, I could spend the crucial days before the trip packing and organizing. I would empty out my hockey bag and carefully pack three sleeping bags, pillows, and a tent. A pot, kettle, and cooking grill were all required and, erring on the side of caution, an axe, hunting knife, first aid kit, and of course my air rifle were all dragged along. Meals were simple. A single can of Zoodles—animal-shaped spaghetti noodles—divided three ways for supper, a cookie or some other sweet for dessert, and hot chocolate to enjoy around the fire before bed.

With everything ready, we would head out in early afternoon, accompanied by our faithful dog, Patch, and walk approximately one kilometre to our destination. Mom and Dad would always offer to drive us across the fields to the camping spot, but I would hear nothing of it. I insisted that my sisters follow me along an overgrown skidder trail through a mosquito-infested spruce forest, dragging half their body weight in unnecessary camping gear. With military precision, Colleen and Erin would trudge obediently behind me while I fearlessly guided them to our predetermined destination. Upon arriving at the selected clearing, the girls would scamper around collecting firewood while I assembled our tent and prepared our beds. With the work out of the way, we would explore the nearby creek, searching for tadpoles, frogs, or other signs of life that inhabited the swampy waters.

The discovery of each frog was reason for celebration as we giggled in amazement at the wonderful creatures that shared our backyard. I would push my way through the cattails, balancing precariously upon the mounds of earth pushed skyward by the hooves of cattle. I scanned the soft mud below, looking for the tracks of wild animals, desperately hoping to uncover evidence of some wild beast, thereby justifying my gun. Meanwhile, Colleen and Erin, oblivious to the potential danger lurking behind every tree, collected bouquets of brilliant yellow swamp lilies, buffalo beans, and fragile bluebells. Looking back, it is amazing they survived.

As evening approached, supper preparation began. I would assemble the cooking grill, which consisted of an old oven rack I had found in the nearby municipal dump, and four metal legs, which I had fashioned from the remnants of a discarded clothes stand. Beneath the grill, a fire was carefully constructed. A tepee of small, dry twigs was carefully placed around a handful of parched moss. With anticipation, I would slowly direct a lit match toward the waiting fuel. With a brief puff of smoke, a fire would begin to crackle. Once burning, larger sticks would be added until a blazing fire roared beneath the grill. The pot was placed upon the grate and the contents of the Zoodles can were added. Together we would sit huddled around the pot, taking turns stirring the mixture and waiting for the surface of the tomato paste to break with a bubble, confirming that supper was ready. After the steaming mixture was poured carefully into three bowls, we would slowly slurp down the delicious contents. Each mouthful was savoured as we gleefully pronounced to each other how a fire really improved the taste. With the Zoodles consumed, the kettle was placed upon the grill and left to boil while we sought out cups, spoons, hot chocolate, and, if Colleen had been clever enough to think of it, marshmallows. Together we would sit around the fire, sipping our sweet drink and enjoying the fresh air until finally it was time to crawl into bed and fall asleep with Patch, our fearless blue heeler, watching over us.

While finishing supper during one of our annual summer excursions, we suddenly noticed the sound of an approaching vehicle. A field bordered our favourite camping spot approximately two hundred metres to the south, and it was possible to turn an automobile off the highway and drive into the field. Given our proximity to town, it was not uncommon for high school students to drive into this field to party. Our eyes grew large with anxiety as we lowered our bowls and strained our ears. The vehicle stopped and its driver killed the engine. The unmistakable creak of a truck door opening and the subsequent slam of its closing echoed across the calm summer night. We looked at each other, terrified. Was someone coming to our spot? What would they do when they got here?

The girls looked to me for leadership. What to do? We would never be able to run home in time. If we stayed, they may discover us. If discovered, they may decide to amuse themselves by forcing us to drink beer, listen to Satan's music on the radio, or, heaven forbid, dance, all of which offended our strict Pentecostal upbringing. Things looked very grim indeed.

With my bravest voice, I ordered the girls into the tent. "Don't say a word," I commanded. "Just sit quietly and wait until I give the all clear."

I scurried outside and quickly gathered the axe and my hunting knife, then threw myself back into the tent and with a knowing look handed the axe to Colleen and carefully placed my hunting knife in Erin's trembling hand. "Only use them if absolutely necessary," I cautioned. I dashed outside once more, zipped the tent up snugly, and sat motionless for a brief moment, straining to hear if the visitors had continued toward us. A muffled laugh erupted from across the meadow. Oh sweet Lord, they were almost upon us. Selflessly I ordered Patch to stay and protect my helpless sisters, and then I slipped into the forest, pellet gun in hand.

Using my self-proclaimed expert hunting skills and taking full advantage of my (imagined) ability to silently stalk prey, I proceeded to intercept the pagans before they reached our secluded encampment. My heart pounded as I raced through the forest toward the field. Surely, I reasoned, they would walk along the trail into the meadow and then follow the natural flow of the land toward us. It was necessary then to hurry through the forest that surrounded the meadow and quietly circle around behind them. Once behind them, I would remain hidden by the trees and further evaluate the situation. If necessary, I could fire a warning shot at their feet or, if warranted, bury a pellet in an unsuspecting bottom. Onward Christian soldier, I was at war.

As I came up behind them I was able to make out the profile

of two human figures. My heart pounded with anticipation. I threw myself to the ground and wriggled through the under-brush toward them. Straining to focus, I guided my air rifle to my shoulder and fixed my sight upon the larger of the two. Another laugh escaped from the bigger visitor. It sounded strangely familiar. With immediate clarity, I realized the two approaching figures were our parents. Even more immediately I remembered I had left my two young sisters armed with sharp and dangerous tools back in the tent with orders to maim first and ask questions later.

I shot up from my position and frantically raced back toward the tent. Breathing hard as I reached our shelter, I fell to my knees and slid to the door. In an instant I ripped open the flap and reached for the weapons sitting awkwardly in my sisters' hands while explaining it was only Mom and Dad who had, unexpectedly, come for a visit. Relieved and embarrassed, we emerged in unison to be greeted by Dad bellowing a jovial hello.

Together the five of us sat around the fire and exchanged stories until the sun fell below the trees. As darkness approached and the fire sputtered and died, my parents said their goodbyes and the three of us squeezed into the tent made for two and drifted off to sleep as faithful Patch stood guard at the door.

CHAPTER 4
RAFTING

As a young child, and continuing until early adolescence when I concluded I was too old for such things, rafting was among my favourite springtime activities. Rafting was only available for that short window of time when the melting snow accumulated within low spots faster than the sun could evaporate the pooling water, so I was always anxious to maximize the limited opportunity. After chores on a warm spring day, I would rush to the largest puddle on our farm where a raft sat waiting on the edge. My rafts were a motley assortment of old boards and posts salvaged from discarded fences and buildings throughout the winter. In spring, the pieces were painstakingly fashioned together, each cut and nailed onto the two largest logs that I was able to drag to my construction site. If I was especially fortunate, Dad would supply me with empty chemical jugs, which were fastened underneath the craft, greatly increasing its buoyancy. I would spend weeks working on a single raft. Dad was always very astute at understanding that it was important to me to design and build my own projects and he would rarely offer, and never impose, his assistance.

As a child of seven or eight, it could take me an hour or more to measure, cut, and nail a single plank to my raft, but when it was done it was mine; I had made it without anyone's help. When it was completed, I would stand back from my creation and gaze proudly at the fruits of my labour with immense pride and satisfaction.

When the time came to put the craft to sea, I would tie discarded baler twine around the support beam specifically designed for that purpose and begin to drag the boat several hundred feet to the largest puddle in the yard. One year I built a particularly large raft and, after several hours of pulling with all the strength I could muster, I realized that, at my current pace, the puddle may evaporate before I could bully the raft to the water's edge. Too stubborn to ask Dad for assistance, I ran and found three fence posts and dragged them to the waiting raft. I placed one post snugly against the front of the raft and pulled the craft up onto it. I was then able to roll the raft forward, place the other two posts beneath it, and roll the raft across the soggy barnyard by returning each post to the front of the raft as it was spit out the back.

Upon reaching the edge of the chosen puddle, I would force the reluctant craft into the water and hold my breath, waiting to see if it would actually float. They always did, some with more confidence than others. With a broken hockey stick in hand, and brimming with the poise and coolness that all boys in knee high rubber boots feel near a puddle, I would step aboard and push off as my chest filled with pride. My sisters and I spent every spare moment, for as long as the puddle remained, floating around the manure-stained waters. Laughing, splashing, marvelling at how deep the water was, and threatening to push each other off.

Unfortunately, my sisters generally got bored with pursuits such as rafting much quicker than I. The challenge then became to find ways in which to entice them to come back and join me for yet another rafting adventure. One sunny Saturday morning, I had an exceptionally brilliant idea: lawn chairs. How did the obvious elude me for so long? A single lawn chair fit perfectly right in the middle of the feeble craft. Now we were rafting in style! I docked and ran to the house to announce the wonderful news.

"Colleen!" I screamed, barely able to contain myself. "I put

31

a lawn chair on the raft! You can now SIT and raft and read and do practically anything!"

It's amazing how a single chair can open up a whole new world of possibilities for a child. Colleen's eyes grew large with excitement as she recognized the creative genius of her brother and she scampered to get her boots on and followed me outside.

Upon returning to the waiting luxury yacht, I graciously allowed her to sit while I chauffeured her around the smelly waters. She was truly impressed with both the comfort and utility of my invention. Beaming, my mind raced to identify additional features of the chair.

"Colleen, you know what else?" I bellowed as if it had been within my contemplation the entire time.

"What?" she fired back in anticipation.

"If you grow tired of floating around and just want to sit and relax, you can anchor yourself to the fence."

To prove I had in fact given this much thought, I directed the raft toward the wooden fence that ran through the middle of the puddle. Once there I hastily pulled some twine out of my pocket and proceeded to tie Colleen and the chair to one of the wooden planks that made up the fence.

"Isn't this great?" I beamed. "Now you can just sit here and relax."

I could tell that Colleen was both impressed and relaxed. Suddenly, I realized the evil genius of the situation. My sister was tied to a chair, the chair was tied to a fence, but the chair was not tied to the raft. If, for some unexpected reason, the raft was to float away, the chair and its occupant would not follow.

With a gentle push, I stepped off the raft and began to shimmy my way down the fence toward dry ground. An intelligent child, Colleen soon realized the seriousness of her situation. The raft was slowly floating away from beneath her and, short of intervention by some caped superhero, she would soon be waist deep in poop water.

Alas, Superman did not heed her calls. With a splash and plenty of crying, Colleen plummeted into putrid, icy waters. At least she was sitting comfortably on the chair.

I relished the pure joy of the situation for a few glorious seconds before returning along the fence to rescue poor, helpless Colleen.

"What happened?" I asked, pretending to be completely clueless as to how such a tragic event could have occurred.

Through tears Colleen explained how the raft had floated away from under her. As any good brother would, I quickly untied her and accompanied her back to the house before she caught cold from her wet clothes.

Poor Colleen deserved better, she was such a dutiful sister. This was the girl who at four years of age used to make me a "lunch" of processed cheese, lovingly cut into small squares and carefully packed within a discarded Strepsils tin, lest I starve to death while playing with my toy tractors. Colleen had noted that Dad always took a lunch to the field when he left for the day so she was not about to let her brother descend into the rumpus room to guide his die-cast model tractors upon the braided wool rug without food to sustain him. Even better than that, when my imaginary field work involved working late into an imaginary night little Colleen would flick off the basement lights on my command and shine a flashlight as directed so I could continue with my play among the glow of fictional headlights. One would hope that such devotion and thoughtfulness would have saved Colleen from and unwelcomed and unexpected bath in a spring puddle, but boys will be boys.

CHAPTER 5
THE CHICKENS

Each spring brought rejuvenation and new life to the farm. As the warm sun began to melt the snow, buds formed on the ends of branches, green grass started to emerge from the earth, and the barns would begin to fill with clumsy calves frolicking in the straw. About the time when the chirping of freshly hatched barn swallows could be heard begging among the rafters, it was time to purchase our annual flock of chicks. After carefully cleaning a small wooden granary, hanging the necessary heat lamps from the ceiling, and laying a neat covering of newspaper on the floor, the family would pile into our old Ford station wagon and make the journey to Smith's hatchery in nearby Prince Albert. There waiting for us were 125 chirping yellow bundles in a large rectangular cardboard box divided into four compartments to ensure the little birds did not suffocate each other in their obvious excitement.

With care, Dad would place the box in the back of the car as my sisters and I would marvel with excitement at the sound of hundreds of little feet scratching against the cardboard. As we drove home, the chicks would voice their discontent with fast corners or rough terrain, breaking into a united chorus of complaint.

Once home, the lid would be pulled back to reveal a swarming yellow mass with tiny orange beaks and large black eyes. One by one, we would reach into the box and gently lift the weightless chicks from their confines and release them into their warm, clean home. Most would hit the ground with their little legs flailing and dash to the nearest corner, pushing together with the others in hopes of finding safety within the group. To keep them from trampling one another, I would gently sweep them out of the corners with my open hand, encouraging them to explore their new surroundings. Slowly but surely, the chicks would gain their confidence and begin to investigate the granary. Stretching their tiny bodies and craning their necks skyward, the chicks would cautiously step about, twisting and turning as they scouted their new home. My sisters and I would sit among the chicks under the warmth of the lamps and watch them strut about. Placing a few grains of feed in our outstretched hands, we would sit perfectly still, waiting for the peck of tiny beaks. Sometimes they would climb onto our hands, their little feet scratching at our skin as they happily snatched up the feed. It was great fun to park among the chicks, watching them interact with us and with each other. It is hard not to smile, sitting under the warm glow of a heat lamp immersed in the middle of a flock of fluffy yellow chicks. There are few things in life that can bring more pure happiness.

Each morning thereafter, I would hurry out of bed and rush off to feed and care for the chicks before climbing onto the bus and heading off to school. I approached the door with a certain apprehension, as it was common to be greeted by the lifeless body of one or more chicks that had not survived the night, given the birds were very fragile during their first few weeks of life. Sometimes they perished for no obvious reason, but typically the cause was suffocation under the crush of their peers as the harebrained birds packed themselves into corners and crevices, presumably trying to recreate the warm embrace of their absent mothers. If fortunate enough to come across an injured bird before it was too late, I would gather it up and rush it to the house and place it gently within the small cardboard box kept beside the kitchen table for that very purpose.

The box was lined daily with fresh newspaper and included a

small bowl of clean water and a second bowl filled with chicken feed. A lamp hovered over the box with the warmth of the bulb directed toward the injured chick, or chicks, as the case may be. We would nurse the injured back to health within the safety of the box, waiting for them to regain their strength and confidence before reintroducing them to the boisterous coop from which they had been rescued. My sisters and I loved having these temporary pets share our home. Crouching shoulder to shoulder over the box, we would watch them strut about their small home, chirping loudly and furiously scratching at their paper bed, confident something good would come from their efforts. When they were tired from their work, the chicks would huddle together under the comforting glow of the light, dip their heads into their breasts, close their eyes and allow the warmth to coax them to sleep.

As the chicks grew and their soft yellow down was replaced with more durable white feathers, the door of the granary was opened each morning to give the young birds the freedom to explore the yard. Initially they were cautious and suspicious of their newfound independence, reluctant to leave the security of their home. Within a few days, however, they would scramble out into the yard the minute the door was opened each day to scratch at the ground and enjoy dust baths in the sun.

Their diet also changed as they grew. The processed chick feed that had sustained them for the first several weeks of their lives was replaced with "chop," a combination of oats, barley, and wheat that had been crushed into a coarse power by the spinning blades of the mix-mill. Dry chop was dumped into shallow wooden troughs and then soaked with water to create a sloppy stew that the chickens relished. Their favourite treat was, without question, "slop," an assortment of kitchen waste scraped from plates and cooking pots over a series of days until the pail kept under the sink was either overflowing or emanating odours too strong to be tolerated in the house.

Walking toward the chickens with a full pail of slop, I would call, "Here chickee, chickee, here chickee, chickee," beckoning the chickens to come. The birds were quickly conditioned to run stampeding at the call. The sight of more than one hundred gangling, clumsy, clucking chickens frantically running toward you, stumbling over each other and themselves is quite hilarious. The eager birds would run right up to me and cock their heads, trying to get a glimpse of the contents of the pail before it was spilled to the ground.

Once I had a sufficient audience, I would toss the slop to the ground and the chickens would dive in, desperate to lay claim to as much food as possible. Those lucky enough to get hold of a piece of mouldy bread, an apple core, or some other sizeable treat would run away from the group, clutching their treasure in their beak as several other birds gave chase, convinced that anything their cousin was determined to run off with was certainly worth fighting for.

Notwithstanding the fact there was a full trough of grain to eat at any given time, the chickens were never hesitant to wrestle one another for food and could be especially cruel to the weak and sick among them. As I entered the chicken pen one morning, I noticed that several of the chickens had open, bleeding sores on their feet. Standing among them, bewildered as to what could have possibly caused their injuries, the answer soon became evident as a nearby chicken, noticing the blood on the foot of his neighbour, quickly snapped his head downward without hesitation to peck at the wound. This immediately drew the attention of several other nearby chickens and in an instant a handful of birds were chasing after their injured friend, nipping at his bloodied foot while he did his best to hobble to safety. Incredibly, the moment the victimized bird had slipped back within the security of the crowd, it sought out and began pecking at the bloody foot of another chicken.

Horrified, I ran to the house and grabbed Colleen in hopes she could help me make some sense of the situation. Colleen was equally dumbfounded but was in agreement that something had to be done. Fighting back tears, we rushed into the pen and began scattering the obviously insane birds. Hoping some quiet time would bring them to their collective senses, we kept the birds moving, scolding them as we pushed them around the pen. The chickens simply needed a moment to collect them-selves we surmised, so we continued to march them round and round, making an example of any delinquent that attempted a quick nibble of a nearby toe by screaming, "Bad chicken! Bad chicken!" while flailing our arms theatrically. Finally, we nervously stopped the march, letting the birds return to their routine, hopeful that the required lesson had been understood and absorbed. It hadn't. The moment we stood back, they once again began eagerly pecking away at any and all visible wounds on one another.

Desperate, Colleen and I ran to Grandma's now abandoned old house and made our way into her modest former bedroom where we found neatly piled stacks of small rags ideal for make-shift bandages. We gathered up handfuls of the rags and quickly made our way back to the chickens. Colleen immediately began sifting through the strips of old clothing, searching for suitable sizes for bandages, while I scurried about the pen trying to catch an injured bird. Following several unsuccessful attempts, I managed to get hold of a frightened, clucking chicken and pin it under my right arm against my body while my left arm struggled to keep its kicking feet still. While I held our reluctant patient, Colleen carefully tied a piece of a tattered shirt to its feet to serve as both a bandage and makeshift armour. When treatment was complete, the chicken was released back into the general population to hobble around on its makeshift shoes.

One by one we caught and bandaged each and every wounded chicken, and by the time we were finished, there were no less than twenty confused chickens stumbling and tripping around the pen, trying desperately to walk with strips of worn old shirts and pieces of pants tied to their feet.

Having completed our task, Colleen and I sat back and anxiously watched the chickens interact with each other, praying our intervention had been successful. With the open wounds buried beneath bulky bandages, the cannibalism stopped and we breathed a sigh of relief. Curious chickens continued to peck sporadically at the trailing rags as the bandaged victims hobbled by, but without the taste of warm blood to reward the peck, the attacks were less frequent and less severe. We congratulated ourselves on our humanitarian efforts and continued on with our day.

That evening at supper, Colleen and I proudly shared our story of compassion with the rest of the family. Dad chuckled as he listened and, when we were finished, took a pail and filled it with warm water before dumping in several tablespoons of salt and mixing the concoction together.

"Go give this to the chickens, Mark," Dad directed. "When you see the chickens pecking at each other, it means they are low on salt."

I blushed as I took the pail, embarrassed that I had failed to recognize the root of the problem. Colleen and I sheepishly made our way back to the chicken coop and dumped the salty liquid into the water bowls before, once again, capturing each chicken so Colleen could untie the rags from their feet.

◎ ◎ ◎

My affinity for chickens led me to acquire a variety of colourful bantams throughout my youth. A chicken with a strange assortment of feathers was a chicken I wanted, as I loved the contrast such birds created in a coop filled with their pure white cousins. Their meat was tough and gamey, and their diminutive frames resulted in small eggs, but provided I took responsibility for their care, Dad always let me indulge such interests.

Our evening routine included locking the chickens securely in their coop to ensure they would be safe from predators through the night. If we failed to do so, it was more likely than not that we would discover a mess of feathers and missing birds in the morning thanks to an unwelcome visit from a coyote or some other intruder.

Generally, the task was as simple as closing the pen door, as chickens instinctively retire to their roosts as the sun sets. So each night, I would pop my head into the coop, take a quick inventory, and then proceed to shut the chickens in, pending release the following morning.

One warm evening in late spring, I noticed that several of my bantams were unaccounted for. Alarmed, I searched the enclosure thoroughly but without success, so I proceeded to examine the surrounding buildings. From time to time a rebellious bird would roost in a nearby shed, so I carefully scoured each of them to no avail. Scared that some misfortune had befallen my pets, I ran to retrieve Dad from the shop and he willingly left his tools to join the hunt. Having the benefit of experience, Dad headed straight for the large maple tree that bordered the chicken pen and, sure enough, perched high among the branches, were the missing birds, clucking their disapproval at our interruption.

This came as a big surprise to me as I had never known a chicken to fly. Dad, on the other hand, was less amazed and more amused as he stood smiling and chuckling beneath the canopy of branches. The bantams, he explained, were small enough to manage some limited flight and were prone to roosting high in trees if given the opportunity.

"But how do we get them in the coop?" I asked, perplexed, staring at the birds fifteen feet above.

"We don't," was Dad's simple response. "If the birds prefer to spend the night outside in a tree, who are we to judge? Let them be. Last time I checked, a coyote cannot climb a tree."

That made sense to me, so we left them where they sat, and they spent the balance of the summer under the stars, secure among the branches. Our job was to ensure our animals were well fed and safe, not to force conformity with a singular version of such things. Dad was always prepared to adapt his approach when the circumstances called for it. As long as the stated objective was achieved, the road taken to get there was of little consequence.

My daughter Kendall and Anna Marshall, my niece,
the next generation of chicken lovers, Edmonton, 2017

CHAPTER 6
THE TURKEYS

As we began our annual trip to Prince Albert to pick up a new batch of chicks one spring, Dad announced that we were going to try a few turkeys this year as well. My sisters and I were very excited at the news, as any opportunity to introduce new animals to the farm was always welcomed. We quizzed our parents as we drove, wanting to know what turkeys ate, where would they stay, and whether or not they would be mean to the chickens. By the time we arrived at the hatchery, we were beside ourselves with excitement, eager to meet our new pets.

After gathering up a cardboard crate full of chicks, two turkey chicks were selected and placed alongside their much cuter cousins in the box. Even freshly hatched, the turkeys were tall and gangly and towered over the young chickens. As we headed home with our precious cargo, my sisters and I took turns crawling into the back of the station wagon, where the crate had been secured, to stare at the chirping mass through the holes punched in the box, ensuring everybody was behaving themselves as we drove.

In the weeks that followed, yellow down was replaced by white feathers as the birds grew and matured. The turkeys' growth greatly outpaced that of the chickens, however, as their frames rapidly expanded upward and outward, making them several times the size of even the largest chickens in the flock. As the turkeys approached maturity, we began to notice that their disposition was changing. It was as if they were becoming aware of their superior size and strength and starting to realize such attributes could be used for their distinct advantage. Soon the turkeys were prancing about the chicken coop like a gang of thugs, helping themselves to food and water as they pleased and showing little consideration for the much weaker chickens.

I would yell at the turkeys and threaten them with a raised hand when I caught them acting cruelly, but they paid little heed to my scolding and continued with their brazen behaviour. Then one day as I mixed chop and water in the trough with a tree branch, I heard the furious pounding of feet against the hard-packed ground and angry gobbling as the turkeys came charging toward me, intent on running me off. I jumped back, startled by their aggression, and wildly swung my stick toward them, flinging wet chop from the end as the stick whipped through the air. My staff connected with the body of one with a deep, satisfying thud, stopping the attacker in its tracks as it let out a garbled yelp before turning to run off, with its companion in pursuit. I stood momentarily staring at the birds as they fled, still shaking as the adrenaline coursed through my body while I tried to understand the reason for the senseless attack.

From that point on, their aggression continued to escalate, and they never missed an opportunity to intimidate. Each time any of us came anywhere close to their enclosure, one or both would begin to strut with a puffed-out chest, warning the tres-passer to reconsider before charging relentlessly if their threats were ignored.

The chickens and turkeys still had to be fed and watered of course, which guaranteed confrontation at least twice daily. I was ten years old at the time, and while not without fear, quickly learned that a solid clobber with my ever-ready stick was enough to turn the turkeys on their heels. So I held onto a weapon at all times and was careful never to turn my back, at least not unintentionally. Sometimes, when feeling particularly brave and wanting to have a little fun, I would turn away and pretend to be preoccupied and unaware of the fact the turkeys were milling nearby. I would stand and listen, clutching my stick with a wry smile, waiting for the turkeys to take the bait and commit to a charge. It never took long before a fluster of ruffling feathers and fierce gobbling could be heard marking the beginning of their assault as they ran toward me. I would continue to wait, allowing them to close the gap between us as my heart raced and my stomach tightened. Then, when they were within a few feet, and seconds away from digging their sharp beaks into the back of my legs, I would spin around and face the birds with my baton swinging wildly, screeching like a gladiator in battle. The turkeys, and every chicken within twenty feet, would jump back and flee with their heads down in a chorus of frantic clucking as I stood tall, relishing in my small victory and my undeniable toughness.

The turkeys eventually learned that aggression toward me always led to an unfavourable result for them, so over time they began to keep their distance. They would continue to strut and threaten, but never within reach of my stick, preferring instead to attack those less prepared, such as my younger sister Colleen.

Colleen was a sweet girl, who did not have a mean bone in her body. She had heard me speak of the turkeys and their ill temper many times and had experienced it herself when helping with chores. Despite that knowledge, she was more inclined to carry a basket of flowers than a bat and preferred to simply keep as much distance between herself and the turkeys as possible, walking well out of her way to avoid confrontation with the miserable birds.

On one sunny summer day, as Colleen skipped across the yard minding her own business, the turkeys took notice. Without hesitation, the birds puffed out their chests and feathers and ran toward Colleen, gobbling furiously. Colleen froze, paralyzed by fear, as tears began to roll down her cheeks and her knees knocked together. The distance between the turkeys and

Colleen grew shorter with each passing second. Fifty feet, forty feet, the gap narrowed as the turkeys continued to charge furiously while Colleen stood trembling, unable to move. Finally, with the birds only seconds away, Colleen instinctively turned, screaming, and ran from her attackers, searching for refuge and yelling for my help. With her little legs pumping for all they were worth, Colleen made a beeline for the nearby hay wagon and jumped up onto the deck in a single leap moments before the turkeys pounced upon her.

Savouring in their near success, the empowered turkeys gobbled louder and began circling the wagon in endless frantic cycles, one running one way and one the other, stopping momentarily from time to time to attempt the three-foot jump from the ground to the wagon's deck with a violent display of flapping wings and kicking feet. Unable to get their plump bodies airborne, the turkeys continued to run, convinced that the faster they ran and the more menacing they appeared, the greater the likelihood Colleen would surrender and throw herself at their mercy. Colleen was beside herself at this point, now screaming wildly for help as she paced nervously in the middle of the wagon and tears poured unchecked down her face.

From within the barn where I was forking manure out the open door, I finally heard Colleen's desperate cries. I popped outside and listened, trying to determine what was going on. I quickly saw little Colleen screaming upon the hay wagon as the turkeys circled below her. Without hesitation, I grabbed my loaded pellet gun from its perch beside the barn door and sprinted toward Colleen as fast as my legs would take me.

"Get away, get away!" I screamed at the top of my lungs as I ran through the lush summer grass. My heart was pounding and my stomach churned with apprehension as I hurried toward the chaos. Bravery can be a burden at times.

The distance soon closed and I found myself upon the

45

turkeys without a formulated plan. In the madness of the moment, gripped by fear and anger, I discharged my pellet gun in their general direction without success and then began wildly kicking at the large fowl while I yelled and hollered, demanding that they leave my sister alone. Both turkeys soon converged upon me. Bobbing and weaving like boxers in a ring, with their wings spread and chests puffed, they tried their best to scratch and peck me as my scrawny legs flailed recklessly, trying to connect with any part of their bodies. Undeterred the turkeys then attempted to mount an attack on two fronts as one continued to rush at me from the front while the other attempted to sneak up from behind while Colleen continued to scream. I spun and kicked and flailed and screamed, desperate for relief from the beaks and claws I feared would be the death of me. Then I heard barking as our dog Patch came barrelling across the yard, yelping threats. His broad, muscular frame was soon before me and his powerful jaws bit into the backside of the first turkey while the second, recognizing his opportunity had passed, turned in surrender and hurried back toward the safety of the chicken coop. Patch gave chase and I followed behind energized with newfound courage as the wretched birds jumped and squawked before us. We chased after the turkeys, running them back to the coop, wishing a thousand deaths upon them.

Shortly thereafter our wish came true and we had our revenge as the turkeys found themselves on the receiving end of a cleaver. We typically butchered approximately eighty chickens each year in groups of twenty or thirty at a time and Dad designated the turkeys to the next batch, in no small part because of their actions.

We always woke at first light to butcher, hoping to catch the birds while they slept and wanting the job complete before the heat of the day interfered with the process. Rustled from my bed just as the orange sun began to crest over the horizon, I would hurry to dress and then stumble, shivering, across the yard, rubbing the sleep from my eyes as my boots left tracks in the silver dew and the cool morning air bit at my skin.

Mom and I would take turns sneaking quietly into the coop where the sleeping birds sat perched silently upon their roosts. One at a time, we would snatch up unsuspecting birds by their legs and hurry from their home as they dangled upside down and confused from our outstretched arms. Jostled awake they would begin flailing in panic, struggling to break our grip as they clucked and squawked in confusion and fear. My hand would squeeze their legs with all my might as my muscles strained against the weight, desperate to avoid the embarrassment of being responsible for the escape of a chicken. Sprinting, I would deliver the birds to Dad where he stood waiting with cleaver in hand beside a thick spruce stump stained with blood and feathers from times before. I would hand the bird over, and without hesitation or regret, Dad would place the chicken breast down upon the stump. Pushing down on the bird's outstretched legs held firmly within his grip, Dad would propel the chicken's head into the stump, forcing the bird to submit. The moment the squirming stopped the cleaver would come crashing down, severing the head from the body in one clean, fluid motion. In the same instant Dad would toss the chicken onto the damp grass, trying to avoid the blood as it sprayed from the wound before quickly swatting the lifeless head off the stump with the blade of the cleaver so as to ensure it would not interfere with the next victim.

The chicken would hit the ground with legs flailing and stumble, skip, and bounce across the wet ground, streaking the green grass red as its muscles contracted and flung its body recklessly. Paying little attention to the scene, we would continue to deliver chickens to Dad until he told us to stop. Then we would stand back and survey the sight before us. Corpses would be spread out a hundred feet in every direction, many still twitching and scratching as the last of their life left them. Dad was always careful to count, often confirming his number by checking the heads at his feet, to ensure every chicken was accounted for. It was not unusual for one to find its way under a granary or elsewhere out of view and, if the heads did not match the bodies, we would search until the quantities equalled.

When confident all were accounted for, we would load the bodies into the wheelbarrow while Mom ran ahead and began to boil huge pots of water on a propane camping stove in the garage. When the water reached a rolling boil, a single bird would be dipped into the water, immediately filling the air with the pungent smell of hot, dirty feathers. The feathers would cling to the body as the chicken was pulled from the pot, and water would drip to the floor as steam rose from the body. Waiting twine was quickly tied to a foot and the carcass was then hung from the brackets that supported the large overhead garage door. With bare hands, I would begin plucking the feathers, while Mom and Dad dipped a bird for each of them. The three of us would grab at the feathers of our bird as it hung, ripping them from the follicles made soft and weak from the boiling water. Feathers would fall in clumps to the newspaper laid on the cement below and the occasional drop of blood would stain the feathers red as they accumulated at our feet. When the majority of the feathers had been plucked, the naked bird was set aside, and without wasting a moment, we would begin pulling the feathers from another bird. On and on we worked until every feather that could be pulled with our bare hands had been removed.

When all the birds were hanging, Dad would strike a match and fire up a propane blow torch. When the proper flame had been achieved, he would quickly rake the fire over the frame of each dead body, burning the tiny down feathers our fingers had been unable to grasp. Careful not to burn the skin, Dad would move from bird to bird as the stench of burning hair mixed with the musty smell of the steamed feathers.

Once the flame had done all that could be expected, the birds were brought into the house. The sinks and counters were piled high with chickens as Mom assembled stations at the kitchen table. A chicken was placed before each of my sisters and me. We were handed tweezers and instructed to search the bird for pinfeathers or anything else that had survived the boiling, plucking, and fire of the garage. We would carefully examine our birds, searching for the thick, stubborn pinfeathers that continued to cling to the bird's tail and neck. One by one we would yank out the feathers and ensure the birds were completely naked and clean before passing the chicken on to Mom or Dad, who each sat with a razor-sharp knife in hand and a bucket at their feet. They would then inspect the bird once more and if it did not meet their approval, would push the chicken back at us demanding that we try harder. If it was satisfactory, they would quickly make an incision below the tail of the bird and scoop out its guts, reaching their bare hands deep within the cavity to ensure the bird was clean. The liver and gizzard were carefully retrieved from the mass of entrails and placed to the side for Grandma, with the rest of the pale innards slopped into the pail between their feet.

Fortunately, we never forced to eat the gizzards ourselves, but Dad always set some aside for Grandma, letting her believe the rest had been saved and would be consumed by our family. Sometimes Dad would take a gizzard and dissect it into two halves, letting us fumble through the soft, mealy centre to search for stones, bits of glass, and other oddities the chicken had consumed.

When the pasty guts began to overflow the pail, I would hop from my seat, eager for a reprieve from the tedious task of pulling feathers with tweezers, grab the steaming pails, and carry them out to the yard with the dogs and cats happily trailing behind. When I reached the chicken coop, I would call the chickens and they would all come running as I tossed the waste onto the bare ground. The chickens would dive in as eagerly as the cats and dogs, either unaware of the source of the meal before them or simply uninterested in knowing the truth. I do not ever recall putting something before a chicken that it would not eat; they seemed quite content to peck away at anything that resembled food.

Back at the house, each cleaned bird was placed within a thick plastic bag and stacked in the freezer to await selection for dinner or supper as the case may be. We had three large freezers, and by the time we had butchered eighty chickens, a steer and a pig, and harvested the garden, all three were bursting. When the job was complete and the temporary "butcher shop" once again resembled a kitchen, the table was wiped with a soapy cloth before we would all sit to each our lunch, fuelling up for the rest of the day as the damp, dull stench of chicken innards began to dissipate.

CHAPTER 7
THE DUMP

We were not a family that took trips to Disneyland, or anywhere for that matter. The most we could hope for was perhaps one weekend a summer crammed into an unserviced shack at Waskesiu Lake with the promise of a "store bought" ice-cream cone or, perhaps, a game of lawn bowling. That was fine by us; our tastes were simple and it never crossed our minds that we should want for more. Besides, there was always too much work to do to be gone from the farm for long, and Dad would grow anxious if away for more than a couple days.

We were frugal out of necessity, but we also wore it as a badge of honour. Fancy things were for fancy people, and being labelled as "rich" was generally viewed as an insult. With few exceptions, everyone we knew lived modestly. To be clear, the homes of our friends and neighbours were filled with food and love and no one wanted for anything, but just the same, most farmers drove old trucks and dressed their kids in patched jeans, and I never met a farm boy with braces on his teeth no matter how desperately they may have been needed.

Being raised in such an environment creates a certain resilience and deep-rooted fiscal conservatism that is nearly impossible to shake. I still encourage my kids to order water at a restaurant (I mean four dollars for a soda pop, seriously), leftovers are saved until eaten, and I try my hardest not to buy anything unless it's on sale. I also grew up conditioned to see value in things others had rejected as worthless. Fortunately for me, the town dump was adjacent to the southern border of the home section, so there was ample opportunity to put this philosophy into practice.

We loved rummaging at the dump. To us, the dump represented a winning lottery ticket, as you were guaranteed to walk away with something every time—it was only a question of how big the prize would be. To be clear, garbage is garbage. We did not haul home crap and we were most definitely not hoarders (despite the evidence I have provided to the contrary), but if we saw a use for something, we took it. A discarded board could still be used to fix a fence or, if nothing else, be burned in the water trough to keep the ice at bay once any and all nails had been salvaged; an old pail might have enough life to act as a receptacle for weeds pulled from the garden; and worn-out jeans made great rags for the shop. As children, my sisters and I would drag such things home behind our bikes, beaming with pride at our resourcefulness.

I stumbled upon my most memorable find while wandering among the trash on a lovely summer day. There, laying pristinely among mounds of debris was the entire contents of someone's childhood bedroom. Books and toys and a floral suitcase that looked as new as the day it was purchased sat seductively before me. Clearly the shelves, drawers and closet of some child leaving the nest had been indiscriminately emptied and tossed with little regard to the value of the contents. Sweet Jesus, had they lost their minds? What had they been thinking? My heart was pounding as I grabbed the suitcase and stuffed it full with books and toys before mounting my bike and frantically pedalling home, clutching my find.

Upon arriving at the house, I burst through the door screaming for Colleen and Heather. I thrust the suitcase and its contents before them and then took a triumphant step back while I watched their eyes widen in excitement.

"There is plenty more where that came from!" I announced.

The girls needed no further convincing. We mounted our bikes and, with plastic bags flapping from the handlebars, hurried back to the dump before someone else could loot our loot. We picked through each and every bit of the trash, laughing and joking as we filled our bags with anything we deemed of value. We took trophies for races we had not run, school scribblers with empty pages, and pencils still able to write. Every toy was stuffed into bags, every book salvaged, and then we hurried back home, fearful someone might try to stop us. We understood that what we were doing was not stealing (the fact that lightning from the heavens had not struck us dead was proof of that), but stumbling upon such an incredible find seemed too good not to be bad.

My parents did not encourage their young children to rummage at the dump, but they certainly did not stop us, nor did they suggest there was anything improper with such activities. We were expected to be resourceful and we were conditioned to take advantage of an opportunity when it presented itself. In our version of the world, it was ungodly to waste and clever to save, and we witnessed examples of this behaviour daily, none more so than by my Grandma Hillenbrand.

Grandma was unquestionably the most frugal person I have ever met. This was a lady who stopped getting the local newspaper (at pennies a copy) because she had not finished reading old issues and who refused to buy a new broom notwithstanding the fact the bristles had been reduced to useless stubs and grooves were worn into the wooden handle from use. She saved every single scrap of paper, plastic, and cardboard that entered the house, and if you ever looked into Grandma's storeroom, you would have seen bits of washed cellophane hung to dry, awaiting their next use. Grandma never got a haircut, not ever—she simply put her hair up in a bun—she did not own makeup or other such superficial things, and despite the encouragement of her daughters, she would only reluctantly accept new clothes when her current wardrobe became too threadbare to be worn.

Grandma left the farm and moved into town upon retirement, and every few days she would call Dad to come retrieve
her table scraps for our dogs. Being the dutiful son, Dad would
oblige and would return home with a bag of boiled chicken
bones with every bit of gristle, fat, and marrow already sucked
from the bleached surface. With no nutritional value remaining,
our dogs would give Dad a look that said, "You have got to be
kidding me," and after a quick sniff, wander off, disappointed.

Grandma was fiercely proud of her ability to make do with
less and made no apologies for her penny-pinching ways. Her
stoic determination was a product of a life spent on the farm
and it extended both to her relationship with money and her
approach to work. She was a tireless worker even in her old age.

When well into her eighties, my grandma, a devout Christian,
volunteered to clean the church every Saturday. She would
spend hours meticulously vacuuming, dusting, and scrubbing.
When Grandma showed up one Saturday morning, she discovered that the vacuum would not work. Most people would have
completed the balance of the tasks and left the vacuuming for
another day or perhaps sought out a replacement appliance.
Not Grandma. She was undeterred and simply dropped to her
knees and spent the next several hours scouring every inch of
floor and picking up bits of dirt and debris with her bare hands.
The job needed to be done, so she did it. A broken vacuum was
nothing more than a poor excuse.

There are two types of people in the world: those that bitch
and moan, and those that put their heads down and do the work
that needs getting done. My grandma was firmly entrenched in
the second grouping.

While I do not pretend to be anywhere near as stoic as my
grandma was, we do share certain characteristics that resulted
in a special bond. When I was a young child, one of my favourite
activities was working with Grandma in the garden. Grandma

did not approach the work begrudgingly but rather with a sense of thankfulness that her good health allowed her to contribute and with gratitude for the food that would sustain us. She would work diligently without rest or complaint, and I would hustle at her side, doing my very best to keep up. One time, when I was no more than five years of age, she stopped to watch me and with pride in her eyes commented, "Mark, you are doing such a good job."

Beaming in her praise, I responded, "Grandma, I just love to work!"

Grandma loved re-telling that story and I was always happy to hear it told. It still makes me smile to know that she was proud of me.

Dad with Belle, 1988

CHAPTER 8
CATS AND DOGS

Farm families typically have numerous pets, and we were certainly no exception. Lady, Patch, Fritz, Belle, Blondie, Harry, and Pepsi were just a few of the many dogs that called the farm home. There were several others, and while I do not recall their names, I do remember my sisters' tears when our parents would tell us of their untimely demise. The constant movement of large machinery is a dangerous place for clumsy, inattentive puppies, and many were lost to the wheels of tractors and trucks over the years. If, through a combination of good luck and circumstance, a new puppy happened to survive the precarious first six months, it was usually with us for many years to come, but never once, that I can recall, did any animal die of old age. Reminders of the fragility of life are never far away on a farm.

Patch and Blondie were two of the dogs with us the longest during my childhood. Patch was a stout and powerful blue heeler that my Grandpa Henderson brought from High River, Alberta, as a puppy. Patch was descended from a family of exceptional cattle dogs, and Grandpa was convinced Patch, with such an impressive pedigree, would be a welcome addition to our farm. As a pup, poor little Patch made the ten-hour trip in the back of Grandpa's car, arriving sick and weary at our door. His arrival was a surprise for my sisters and me, and while we were thrilled with our gift, we looked upon Patch with some suspicion and disappointment as we watched this timid little pup throw up on our driveway as he stumbled from the car.

Patch proved to be all that was promised. He was faithful, obedient, and a relentless guard dog. Not a single vehicle, human, rodent, or predator made it onto the yard unannounced in all of his years. Whenever a vehicle turned into our driveway, whether known or not, Patch would lose his mind and tear toward the machine as if the survival of all that was good and decent in the world depended on him intercepting the intruder. Once he caught up to the vehicle, he would run alongside the driver's side door, barking furiously with bared teeth and bristled hair, demanding retreat. When the vehicle ultimately came to a stop, he would jump up and repeatedly pound his front paws into the door while continuing to growl and snarl, flashing his teeth and doing his very best to be menacing. Wisely, even big, burly men would sit securely in their trucks until one of us pulled Patch off the door. Despite this behaviour, Patch never once bit anyone. His intent was never to hurt, simply to protect, and the minute we called him off, he was as friendly and gentle as you could hope.

Aunt Inga, Erin, Mom, Heather, Colleen, Uncle Bill,
Dad, me, Cousin Grant, and Patch, December 1982

Much of his blustering was, of course, just a game to him as he would attack anything with wheels, even if Dad was the operator. When we tried to drive off the yard, whether it be in a car, truck, or tractor, he would run alongside and viciously bite at the tires. He didn't just nip at the wheels, he bit them as hard as he possibility could, desperate to inflict as much pain and suffering upon the inanimate piece of rubber as was earthly possible. More than once, his teeth took such a firm grip that he found himself anchored to the wheel and was quickly slammed to the ground after making a rotation or two. His jaw was strong enough to damage the car tires, so Dad would back out of the garage as quietly as possible before flooring it and speeding toward the highway, while gravel and mud spit out behind us and Patch could be seen barrelling across the yard trying his very best to catch up. Sometimes he would hide around the corner of the garage, waiting for the car to leave. As soon as the forward momentum began he would spring out and run toward the car, biting at the wheels as he followed it down the highway for as long as his short legs would allow.

Big vehicles may have been Patch's favourite, but any wheel would do. Start the lawnmower and here comes Patch, biting at the tires and yanking the mower from your hands. Grab the wheelbarrow, enter Patch. If it turned in a perfect circle, it made him angry. I could only imagine what he would have done had he ever seen a Ferris wheel.

As Patch became older, his vision began to blur and his joints stiffened, making it difficult for him to manoeuvre quickly around machinery. Aware of his state, we were always careful to watch closely for his whereabouts and did our best to protect him. In spite of this, Dad caught his hind legs and torso under the wheel of a tractor when backing up quickly in the tight confines of the calf pen. The injuries were severe and it was clear that Patch could not be helped, so Dad reluctantly went for a shotgun. Unable to bring himself to look at Patch, and not wanting his friend to see him, Dad leaned against the end of a nearby granary, stretched the gun out around the corner and pulled the trigger. It was a difficult thing for Dad to do, but it was a responsibility he knew was his, so he did what he believed to be right.

◉ ◉ ◉

Blondie was a beautiful yellow golden retriever with boundless energy and a sunny disposition. She had a wonderful spirit about her and was a faithful pet for many years.

Returning home from university for a weekend in the dead of winter, I bundled up in my work clothes and hurried outside to help Dad with the chores. As I stepped out through the garage toward the yard, I was greeted by the frozen body of Blondie. From the trail of ever-shortening paw prints in the fresh snow, it was clear that Blondie had stumbled before collapsing to her death. Blondie had been poisoned. I poked my head back into the house and listened for my girlfriend, Kristin, who had accompanied me on the trip, ensuring she was in the living room and away from any windows looking out onto the yard. Confident I was out of her line of sight, I hurried back outside and dragged Blondie's body down the yard and deposited her at the edge of the forest. It was upsetting and disappointing, but the reality of farm life was that you grew accustomed to such things, and as result they become neither surprising nor devastating but were rather accepted as part of life. That is not to suggest we did not grieve loss—we most certainly did, for we loved our pets. I only saw my dad cry a handful of times in my life, and most of them were when a favourite dog died. But farm life is just different. There is a practicality applied to death and a recognition that we have little choice but to move on. After all, the chores still needed to be done.

For every dog we ever owned, we easily had five cats. Black, white, and brown; big and small; short-haired and long; and every combination imaginable at one time or other was part of our brood. Much like the dogs, our cats served as pets but were primarily kept to keep the rodent population under control. With bins full of grain and rows of bales, the farm was an ideal environment for mice and rats, and a handful of cats living in the barns were charged with the responsibility of hunting the unwanted pests.

The cats were generally self-sufficient and had little difficulty staying healthy and plump off the spoils of the farm except during the coldest months when we supplemented their diets with store-bought cat food. Those that were more domesticated than others would lounge around the house on a regular basis, begging for kitchen scraps and searching for our affection. Others, however, looked upon us with suspicion and had their litters under granaries or deep within the woodpile, never allowing us to get too close.

It was incredibly exciting to discover a litter of kittens stumbling out from the woodpile for the first time. I would rush toward them, gasping with glee as they scattered and ran for refuge. It was nearly impossible to catch one, but that fact did not dissuade me. I would crouch motionless behind the nearby water trough, peeking ever so carefully around the corner, waiting for a kitten to emerge so I could spring up and desperately try again to capture the tiny creature. If I was lucky enough to get one in my grasp, I was quickly convinced to loosen my grip when their sharp teeth sank into my fingers while their small claws raked wildly across my skin.

Like the dogs, the cats also found the farm to be fraught with danger. Most were somewhat distant and antisocial, which kept them removed from the general hustle and bustle of moving machinery and the people operating the same. They were also generally more alert and agile, not to mention a much smaller target to hit, so were often able to avoid precarious situations. But the cats were also less loyal and more inclined to wander off the farm, only to fall prey to coyotes, the highway, or the neighbour's dogs.

Two-toes the cat is a sad example of the dangers of farm life. Two-toes (formerly Blackie as practically every black or "blackish" cat was named) was a particularly friendly animal who appeared to be well suited for farm life. He was a respectable mouser, stayed clear of moving machinery, and had the good sense not to wander off the farm. Despite these traits, he obviously failed to grasp basic science.

Two-toes, like every other animal on the farm, drank water from the water troughs. The large metal troughs held several hundred gallons of water. In the winter the troughs were heated by continually stoking a fire contained within the barrel heater at one end of the trough. Despite the presence of a fire, much of the water in the trough still froze like a giant ice cube, leaving open water in the middle of the trough and toward the back, close to the fire. Our cats would jump up on the trough, balance on the icy edge, and carefully lap at the water below them.

On a cold winter night, Blackie had perched himself on the edge of the trough and began to drink. Foolishly, he did not return to the warmth of his heated home immediately after his drink and sat aloft the icy trough, observing the cattle around him while his warm paws settled into the cold ice. To his dismay, he discovered he was unable to leave when he wanted to do so. His paws had frozen into the ice and he was stuck to the trough. The unfortunate creature had no choice but to wait through the night until Dad came out in the early morning to feed the cattle. As Dad approached the trough, the cat began to whine. Concerned, Dad hurried over to the animal, reached down and picked him up to see what was wrong, not knowing, of course, that it was frozen to the trough. The unfortunate result is revealed in Blackie's new name for "Two-toes" spent the rest of his days with only two toes on his right paw.

Dad with Rusty, 1995

CHAPTER 9
WORK AND PLAY

My dad was an exceptional farmer and a tireless worker. When there was a job to be done, he did not make or accept excuses, regardless of the task. In addition to feeding the livestock and tending to the crops, he kept the yard neat and his tools in order. The machinery was well maintained and cleaned regularly. Spilled grain was swept up, busted bales were gathered, and broken branches were piled. If it needed doing, he did it.

At the end of a long day, tired, hungry, and covered in dust and grease, Dad would still take the time to sweep the garage and neatly place his boots and coveralls in preparation for the following morning before coming in the house. He never took a shortcut and he never left for tomorrow what he could accomplish today. When the day was all but over, and he had given all he could, he always did one more thing.

One more load of bales, one more round on the tractor, one more length of fencing. We always pushed to achieve as much as was possible, for Dad understood the correlation between effort and success.

For most, work ethic is a learned behaviour. Without exposure to work and without experiencing the satisfaction of a job well done, many are conditioned to believe work is something to be avoided and fall well short of their potential as a result. My sisters and I were nurtured in an environment in which an individual's work ethic was seen as a critical component of their worth and character. To be labelled lazy was a deep and cutting insult.

As if his own example was not enough, Dad often pointed to our neighbours, Stan and Elvena Zawada, as an example of an exemplary work ethic.

"Those people know how to work!" Dad would proclaim, while pounding a fist on the table for emphasis.

In addition to a large grain and cattle operation, they ran a dairy, sold eggs, and always had some sort of side hustle on the go. They even had the audacity to put their garden (correction, one of their *three* large gardens) right in front of the house so that when people drove by they could witness with their own eyes that Elvena's garden did not have a single weed.

The Zawadas were up with the sun and worked long after it had retired into the horizon. Should we find the need to visit, we never stopped at the house; they could be found in the barn or in the fields, working. I remember being captivated by their entrepreneurialism and boundless energy.

There was nothing particularly unusual about the Zawadas, however. That is how most of the farm families we knew lived, because if you are going to be a farmer, you are going to work hard. The needs of your land and livestock determine the length of your days, for farming is ultimately about stewardship, about caring for the life you have been entrusted with. We worked hard, there is no doubt, but it did not feel like work. We were putting in the hours so the soil would produce and the cattle would flourish. Most importantly, we did it together. The family farm of my generation was just that, a collective pursuit by the family in which the contribution of each was critical to the success of all. It bound us to each other and to the land in ways that cannot truly be understood unless you have lived it.

My earliest memory of working with my dad is from when I was no more than four years old. He took me outside on a cold winter day and stood me beside the throttle in the cab of the Case 830 where it sat parked, hooked to the mix-mill, a large piece of equipment that would grind straw and grain to create a mix of both that the cattle loved.

When Dad waved, I would push the throttle up and he would feed in the bales; when he needed a short reprieve, he would wave again and I would pull the throttle down, waiting for the next signal. I remember returning to the house when the job was complete and standing at the back door in my snowsuit with cold fingers and toes, but beaming from ear to ear while Dad sang my praises to Mom and spoke of what a great help I had been. My role that day was, of course, just busywork, but Dad let me believe I was needed and that I had made a difference.

A family farm allows for those experiences. It lets children organically immerse themselves in work and responsibility so they might discover how gratifying a job well done can be. Try bottle-feeding a motherless calf while it happily slurps at its meal or successfully sneaking a warm egg from beneath a nesting hen. I promise you that both will put a smile on your face and neither will feel anything remotely like work.

While work certainly took priority, that is not to suggest we did not stop to have some fun from time to time. We are, after all, nothing more than a speck in an infinite universe, so it's best not to take oneself too seriously.

For my parents, "fun" was typically coffee with friends, a nice drive in the country, or perhaps a walk about the yard. Dad use to love showing off the yard and his cattle, especially to his siblings when they would come home to visit. We would all head outside for a classic "Hillenbrand walk" around the farm on a lazy Sunday afternoon with Dad leading the pack, beaming proudly as he petted cows or tried to ride a bull while his sisters scolded and his brother encouraged. He knew every cow and every calf and took great pride in making sure they were all enjoying their time in his care.

Dad also found it hilarious to tease our dog Patch, the fierce blue heeler that Grandpa Henderson had brought from Alberta as a pup. For some inexplicable reason Patch would go absolutely crazy when Dad used the air compressor so, when in need of some comic relief, Dad would pull the trigger and shoot random blasts of air and Patch would come running at full speed from wherever he may have been sleeping, yelping madly. Once he reached Dad, Patch would snap wildly at the stream of air as if possessed while Dad laughed uncontrollably. Dad even kept a discarded length of rubber hose by the compressor that he could shoot air through while Patch bit and pulled at the hose, thereby enhancing their game.

Our entertainment was never flashy or expensive and could be found in the simplest of things. When Dad wanted to hear "Oh Lord It's Hard to Be Humble" on the jukebox in a small café in Duck Lake, Saskatchewan, after a day of touring the site of the Riel Rebellion, he plunked in a quarter and made the selection. Then we all sat and patiently waited while Dad crouched in anticipation with his ear turned toward the speaker, telling us all with confidence, "Just one more. It's going to be the next song; I just know it!" His joy in such simple things brought us joy, and we all found happiness in seeing him smile.

For us kids, fun was almost always found outside, and one of our favourite places to play was among the bales. Square bales, approximately eighteen inches wide and thirty-six inches long (give or take) were essentially oversized Lego blocks that could be assembled in any variety of ways to construct forts or elaborate mazes. The large round bales, standing six feet high or more, and often stacked two to three bales high, made for a fabulous playground within which to play tag, hide-and-go-seek, or king of the mountain.

I recall playing on the bale stack in first grade with Heather and a friend on a sunny winter day. Perched at the very top, I peered over the edge and noticed that the protruding bales below created a ledge. How perfect, I thought, I can jump off and land on the ledge, yet lead Heather to believe I have plunged twenty feet to my death!

If my plan was going to have the biggest theatrical impact I would need to play this up, so I instructed Heather to pretend to shoot me and, upon hearing "bang," I planned to shock them both by carefully jumping to the safety of the ledge below.

Heather was happy to accommodate. Wonderful, I thought, as I turned my back and prepared myself.

"Okay, I'm ready!" I announced.

I then heard Heather yell "bang" directly into my ear, and before I had an opportunity to implement my scheme, I felt her hands slam forcefully into my back. I screamed while I passed by the ledge and then screamed some more as I crashed into a snowdrift below. I gathered myself up and let Heather know in no uncertain terms that she could have killed me. I am not sure she could hear me above their laughter.

The dugout also provided an endless source of entertainment.

The dugout was sixty feet across and close to two hundred feet long with steep hills of deposited dirt on either side. In the winter we would sled down those hills or shovel off the surface to skate, and in the summer it provided a perfect spot to skip rocks or try our hands at fishing. There were most definitely no fish in the pond, but that did not deter us; the mere possibility that there might be was reason enough to try. We also attempted swimming in the muddy waters on a few occasions. The water was rank, filled with algae and the smells and deposits of cattle. The bottom was a mixture of clay and slop that pulled at your ankles and slurped in resistance as you tried to move along it. No reasonable person would have entered the water, but Dad claimed he regularly swam in the dugout as a child, and if he had, so would we.

To be fair, we never ventured in past our waists so to say we "swam" in the waters is perhaps a bit of a stretch. We were adventurous and bold, but that is not to say we were stupid or particularly enthused about the possibility of gulping down a mouthful of cow-poop water. Swimming in the dugout was mostly about showing off to friends, to whom we no doubt embellished our cautious wading with stories of multiple laps, and so we might be able to claim a shared experience with Dad. After all, we knew we would never be permitted to fire live rounds at each other with a .22 rifle as Dad bragged was a regular occurrence between himself and his brother Manfred. We had to take what we could get.

Then there was the time our hired man Delbert showed up with a motorboat. He had bought a small aluminum fishing boat and insisted on taking us for a ride in the dugout. Why in the world Dad ever indulged such ridiculous activities is beyond me; Lord knows I do not have that kind of patience. But Dad could see how excited Delbert was, so he helped him back the boat and trailer as close to the pond as possible, and the two of them manhandled the small craft into the water. We climbed into the boat, and with a smile that took up the entirety of his face, Delbert fired up the motor and floored it. Delbert was never one to take it easy in such situations.

The boat burst forward as the sounds of the straining motor echoed off the dugout walls and we were thrown back off the bench seat, laughing with fear and excitement. As quickly as he had hit the throttle, Delbert was forced to back off the gas and manoeuvre the tight turn lest we go flying into the cattails and sedges beyond the water's edge. Once turned and facing the opposite direction, he would hammer the throttle once more, flinging us toward the opposite shore as we screamed in glee at our three-second boat ride.

As young children, hide-and-go-seek, kick the can, and sardines (in which you hid with the person designated as "it," once found) were favourite games to play when company was over, especially at night when the cover of darkness added a level of mystery and danger. As we aged, our recreation often involved target shooting with guns or exploring the surrounding fields and forests on motorbikes and snowmobiles. We had a tremendous amount of freedom, and few limits were placed on what we could or could not do. "Be home for supper and do not be stupid" were the basic expectations. As a teenager, it was not unusual for me to spend an entire Sunday (after church and chores, of course) exploring the countryside on my motorcycle many miles from home. I would drive until I judged my fuel to be half gone and would then turn around and make my way back. There was no "checking in" via text or otherwise; we were just turned lose into the world and left to take responsibility for ourselves.

As we moved into our late teenage years, a favourite Saturday night pastime was "haunted housing," in which we would gather with friends and drive lonely dirt roads until coming upon an

abandoned homestead. With quickly invented claims of haunt-
ings and all matter of horrific events, we would exit the vehicle
and make our way through the dark and empty house, seeking
an opportunity to scare each other with screams and well-timed
punches. I remember one instance in which a particularly bold
friend quickly separated from the group and disappeared up the
stairs in a dilapidated two-storey house. He proceeded to let
rip a series of bloodcurdling screams before hiding silently in
the darkness of a closet, leaving us to determine whether the
display was a trick or if real harm had come to him. We were
pretty confident it was the former, but only when we began
to drive off, leaving him to walk the many miles home did he
reveal himself.

It was all so much fun and I cannot imagine any better way
to be raised. We were never bored. We never uttered the words
"there is nothing to do." There was always an adventure waiting
beyond the front door and we were given the independence to
go find it.

CHAPTER 10
BRINGING IN THE COWS

The cattle would come home from the pasture each fall shortly after the first hard frost, once they had picked the last of the summer grass and found every bit of grain spilled during the harvest. Standing at the gate leading into the corral, they would announce their arrival in an endless chorus of moos and bawling, waiting to be fed in the familiar surroundings of the yard. They were a motley bunch, made up of a combination of Charolais, Hereford, Angus, Simmental, and Salers—a sea of white, black, red, brown, and every conceivable combination thereof.

We would oblige their wishes, rolling out bales of hay and spreading straw among the barn and windbreakers to provide a warm, dry bed. Dad would stand a half dozen or more large round bales upright around the corral and within the large red barn that housed the cows. I would then cut the twine and pull it off so as not to litter the ground and tempt a curious calf to its detriment. With the string off, I would pull away as much of the outer layers of straw as was necessary to decrease the bulk of the bale to the point where I was able to push it over on its side and roll it out like a giant cinnamon bun. My forearms and shoulders would burn in pain as I pulled apart bale after bale, throwing huge, heavy forks full of straw about the barn, working to create a uniform and comfortable bed for the cattle to rest.

Before I was deemed old enough to handle a knife to cut the string, I would simply find the end of the twine where it lay loose against the bale. Gathering it up, I would then walk around the bale in the opposite direction, pulling the string away from

71

the feed and wrapping it between my thumb and elbow while simultaneously shooing and pushing the eager cattle out of my path as they tried to bully their way to the front of the line. Alternatively, I would wrap the twine around the glove on my left hand as I hurriedly yanked it off with my right. This method resulted in a thick, tight ball of twine encapsulating my hand and creating a deformity that I found quite amusing as a ten-year-old boy. To remove the string, I would collapse my hand within the glove and wiggle my hand free, leaving my glove at the core of the ball. With the tension released, the glove would slide free and the twine could be disposed of.

The problem, of course, was that after a few rotations of the twine around my hand I was essentially anchored to the thousand-pound bale. This would be of little consequence if dozens of cattle were not milling around, trying to sneak a mouthful of feed before my job was done. I remember on one occasion as a child when, frightened by the aggressiveness of the cattle, I backed away from the bale, leaving a gap between the bale and myself. An excited calf quickly ran between and in an instant the twine was wrenched tight against my hand and I was thrown to the ground and dragged along the frozen earth. I bounced off frozen cow patties and through a couple unfrozen ones for a few frightful seconds before the string snapped, freeing me from the unwelcome ride. As I picked myself up, checking for broken bones and bruises, I made a decision to discontinue my practice and find other ways to gather up twine.

After the cattle had been given a few days to adjust to life within the corrals, we would begin the process of weaning the calves. Dad would grab a couple five-gallon pails filled with grain and walk into the corral calling, "Come Boss, come Boss," in a deep, authoritative voice. The cows would immediately perk to attention and turn their heads toward us. They realized something was afoot but were not yet convinced it was worth getting up for. Holding a single pail high into the air for all to see, Dad would tease the cattle by allowing a bit of the grain to spill onto the ground with an exaggerated motion. It worked every time. The cattle stampeded over, each trying desperately to be the lucky one that got a mouthful of grain. By this point, Dad had jogged away another twenty or thirty feet in the direction of an open gate leading into a separate corral and was again shaking out a small bit of grain onto the ground while continuing to call, "Come Boss, come Boss."

Convinced the next pile had to be bigger, the cattle collectively swarmed toward Dad and hastily licked up the new deposit of grain. And so the process continued and the trap was laid. By the end, the smarter cows were bobbing their heads into the pails as Dad held them secure, while the rest continued to scurry from one pile to the next, connecting the dots that led them all through an open gate and into an adjacent corral.

The calves, meanwhile, had ignored the event for the most part or, at best, lagged behind, understanding the futility of trying to compete with their greedy mothers for grain. With the security of a large stick and a yapping dog, I would stand at the entrance to the corral like a bouncer, shooing aside the minors that tried to sneak past while letting the cows through.

Within a half hour or so, the unsuspecting cows had been separated from their calves and locked within the holding pen. The confused calves were then hurried across the yard into the waiting calf pen, which was to become their home for the next six to ten months while they fattened for market. Shortly thereafter, they all realized they had been duped and panic set in. The cows frantically paced along the fence with their heads tilted back, screaming for their young while their calves did the same in an endless chorus of bawls. The sound of dozens of disgruntled animals letting their displeasure be known could be deafening and would continue for days as the cattle pleaded

73

for a reunion. I remember feeling pangs of sympathy, imagining how difficult it would be to be instantly orphaned. Fortunately, their pain was short lived, as within a few days all but a few stragglers had accepted their fate and were contently going about their business.

For the unfortunate calves, the unpleasantness was not yet over. After the stress of separation from their mothers had subsided, we would begin the process of treating them.

The calf pen consisted of two distinct halves separated by a gate. All the calves were chased into one half of the corral and the gate closed behind them. More manageable groups of six to ten calves each were then directed into an adjacent holding pen that funnelled into a narrow wooden chute built from heavy spruce boards and thick posts. By a clever combination of forks, yelling, electric cattle prods, barking dogs, and tail twisting, the reluctant calves were persuaded down the chute single file. Once in the gangway, a post would be quickly slid horizontally behind the calf's rump and left to rest on the two parallel planks making up each side of the chute. Braced against opposite posts, the pole blocked the calf's retreat, leaving it with no escape.

That is not to say they would not try. Many would desperately attempt to contort their bodies, straining against the sides in hopes of walking out the same way they came in. Others would attempt to jump over the walls, fearful of what was awaiting them at the end of the line. They had good reason to be afraid. At the end of the gangway, a headgate was firmly fastened and chained to two large posts.

The headgate was built of thick, tubular steel welded and bolted together much like the jaws of giant pliers. One of the arms was secured to the frame, while the other pivoted on a pin anchored to the base. A string was tied to the top of the swinging arm and, as the head of each animal passed through, it was yanked hard and fast, collapsing the locking jaws around the neck of the animal and securing its head in place.

Each animal approached the headgate differently. Some would charge at it, kicking and snorting with great theatrics, refusing to submit to our will. The posts would shudder under their weight, and the steel would rattle and clang as bone and muscle met metal. Others would sneak up slowly. Certain they could outsmart the contraption and escape to the comfort of the familiar pen beyond, they would pounce at the last moment in an attempt to sneak through the gap. Still others would simply walk right in without the slightest concern.

One by one each calf would take its turn, so an examination could be performed. First, Dad would check for any ailments that required medicine of one sort or another. If the calf had one or more eyes swollen, pink eye was diagnosed and medicine was sprayed into the eye while the animal squirmed in discomfort. If its nose was running and its breathing was laboured, we would grab the animal's head and force it back before ramming large sulfur boluses down its throat at the end of a long plunger designed for that purpose. If an unappreciative calf spit them up, we would collect them from the ground, splash a little water over the large pills to wash off all straw, snot and manure, and then defiantly force them back down the animal's throat, forcing the calf to swallow. The pills were too expensive to waste, and we certainly were not about to reward an animal for bad behaviour.

Every horn was cut. Cattle with horns were subject to a small deduction at market. Further, those animals with horns had a distinct advantage over those without in the daily squabbles over food and shelter that went on among them. To encourage peace within the herd and maximize the profit on our investment, all horns were cut. This was done in one of two ways. If the horns were relatively small, we would clip them off in one quick motion using a dehorner, a large, heavy tool consisting of two long handles leading to a mechanism of dual V-shaped, cleaver-like blades and gears. When the handles were pulled apart, the blades would separate, leaving a gap between. A horn would be directed into the void and, when the tool was properly lined up to ensure the horn would be cut cleanly, the handles would be forced together in one fluid, powerful stroke, clipping the horn from the calf's head. As the horn popped off, a stream of hot red blood would shoot from the fresh wound and cover anything in its path. After a day of cutting horns, everything, including our clothes and faces, were painted with streaks of salty blood. Needless to say, it was not a particularly pleasant experience for the calves.

With a larger animal, the risk of excessive bleeding necessitated the use of a wire cutter, which would cauterize the wound as it cut through the horn. A single wire the thickness of a strand of spaghetti was anchored between two small rods of stainless steel, each a couple inches long, providing handles to grip at each end of the two-foot wire. The wire was then placed against the horn and drawn back and forth across it in long, heavy strokes as a tiny whisper of smoke rose from the cut and the smell of burning hair and flesh filled our nostrils. It was hard, dirty, dangerous work as the cattle did their best to slam their heads into our bodies in hopes of weakening our resolve. Sweat would fill my eyes as I strained against the horn, pulling as fast and as hard as I could, slowing only when the horn began to give. Then I switched to small, gentle strokes so as not to injure the animal and ensure a clean finish.

Castration was equally messy and unpleasant. Each young bull calf had to be castrated to reduce its testosterone. Less testosterone meant a better-quality meat and, perhaps more importantly, would ensure the young bulls did not waste all of their energy fighting over and chasing the heifers all day long.

While still in the headgate, Dad would climb into the chute

behind the nervous young bull while I stood above the animal with my feet braced on the planks on either side of the animal, much like a bull rider before mounting his ride. Grabbing the tail, I held it up and out of the way, pulling up with as much strength as possible without lifting the calf off the ground. If the tail was held properly and at the correct angle, the back legs of the calf would be rendered temporarily paralyzed, minimizing the number of kicks Dad would have to endure.

Reaching into the bucket of warm, soapy water between his feet, Dad would throw a few handfuls of water onto the calf's scrotum to disinfect the area in preparation for surgery. Dad would then grab the animal's testicles in one hand and yank down firmly. With a quick flip of the wrist he would slice into the scrotum with a scalpel, forcing the first testicle out of the pouch and exposing the cord. A quick cut and the freed testicle was tossed aside to a waiting dog who would happily gulp down the meal in a single swallow. Without missing a beat, the second testicle would be popped from the incision in the scrotum, the cord cut, and again tossed to the dog who was thrilled to have a second helping. A few more splashes of water onto the open wound and the animal would be released from the headgate back into the first pen to carefully sit on the thick layer of fresh straw we had prepared for them.

We were not without sympathy for our cattle. Notwithstanding the crude operating theatre and our rudimentary veterinarian practices, we were always careful to do what we could to minimize the suffering our animals had to endure. The cattle were always well fed and sheltered, and carefully observed for signs of sickness. Content, healthy cattle did, after all, gain more weight and fetch higher prices at market. But horns had to be cut and bulls converted to steers. It was simply the way it was, the way it had always been, and the way it will always be on the farm.

◎ ◎ ◎

I remember vividly the first time my young sisters watched a steer being butchered. They stood excitedly on the fence, realizing what was about to unfold, but not truly understanding it as Dad and I cornered the apprehensive yearling. Once the animal was calm and still, Dad took a few cautious steps toward it while raising the single shot .22 calibre rifle we always used on such occasions. In an instant, and seemingly without warning, the crack of the rifle could be heard echoing through the yard as the bullet met its mark. Life left the animal in the same second as its legs collapsed beneath it, and it landed with a heavy thud.

Throwing down the gun, Dad rushed toward the animal with butcher knife in hand while I followed with chains. As Dad quickly slit its throat, I wrapped a chain around the still quivering back legs and then hooked the opposite end to the bucket of the tractor Dad was then lowering over the animal. Within thirty seconds from when the trigger was pulled, the animal was dangling high into the air while blood spilled from the open wound on it neck.

My now-terrified sisters gripped the fence and cried uncontrollably at what they had just witnessed. I remember Dad's frustration as he ordered them to the house. He was not angry at them for their reaction, but with himself for permitting them to experience something so upsetting when they were clearly too young to understand and accept the process.

We would then proceed to gut and skin the animal in the far corner of the yard before leaving the carcass to age, hanging among the tools and equipment in the machine shop. Our hope was to age a carcass for three weeks before dividing each side of beef into steaks, roasts, and hamburger; however, the length of the aging process was ultimately determined by the weather. Butchering occurred in mid-spring, when the weather would turn the shop into a natural fridge as temperatures hovered just above freezing. If the days become unseasonably warm, we would be forced to pile snow around the hanging beef to afford a few more days before we would gather as a family and tackle the processing together.

I took no pleasure in butchering, castration, and the like, but I never felt remorse for such things either. It was all part of the job, just another chore that needed to be completed. I wanted to help and learn and be a part of each and every task undertaken each and every day, and I never shied away from any job, no matter how unpleasant.

● ● ●

Like my sisters, my wife, Kristin, experienced a harsh initiation to some of the less delicate aspects of farm life. Her first visit, early on in our relationship, was in February during the height of calving season.

Dad returned to the house one evening after checking the cattle and announced a cow was calving, should she wish to watch. With a smile that appeared sincere, she happily responded that she would love to.

After bundling Kristin up in my mom's farm-friendly fashions, the three of us headed out into the darkness. Following the bouncing glow of Dad's flashlight as the snow crunched beneath our feet, we trudged along the slippery path to the old log barn where the labouring cow was waiting.

At that time the log barn was the only original building still standing on the yard. Approximately twenty feet wide and forty feet long, it was constructed some eighty years previously from spruce logs harvested on the farm. It had a certain comforting charm and was filled with history. It is quiet, cozy, and warm. The hand-hewn mangers are well worn, oily, and smooth to the touch from decades of livestock leaning in to feed. Dusty, brittle leather harnesses still hang from the support beams despite the fact horses have not been kept on the farm in more than thirty years. Most of the wooden floor has rotted away, leaving bare earth, and much of the cement packed between the cracks of the logs has broken free and fallen to the ground allowing slivers of light illuminating from the single bulb dangling from the ceiling to seep out into the night.

As we pulled back the heavy wooden door and stepped into the warmth of the barn, it was clear the cow was having difficulty with her delivery. Only a few inches of one of the calf's hooves was protruding from its mother, and little progress had been made since Dad left her. As Kristin stepped into an adjacent stall and peered cautiously between the fence planks, Dad and I began to work at pulling out the calf.

A lasso was retrieved from a large wooden dowel sticking out from a support pillar and tossed around the neck of the cow. We met with little resistance from the exhausted mother, as she was too tired to struggle. I secured the animal to the nearest post and grabbed a stainless-steel chain two feet in length from the pail of warm water we had carried with us while Dad took off his jacket and rolled up his sleeves. I handed Dad the chain and braced myself against the animal to help keep her on her feet and discourage resistance while Dad slid a hand holding the now looped chain into the animal, attempting to locate the feet, which had now retreated inside the womb.

Struggling to locate a single hoof, Dad manoeuvred his arm deep within the cramped quarters until the chain was successfully wrapped around an ankle of the calf. After he pulled out his arm, we each grabbed onto the free end of the gooey, slippery chain and pulled with all our strength until one of the calf's legs was protruding eight inches from the back end of its mother.

I held the chain tight, being careful not to let the leg retreat, while Dad repeated the process with a second chain, locating the other hoof. Once the second hoof was anchored, we yanked it forward until both feet were an equal distance out of the animal. After giving both the labouring mother and ourselves a few moments to catch our breath, we began to pull with as much strength as we could muster, bracing our feet and straining our backs as we worked to deliver the calf. Much to our relief, the head and shoulders soon popped free. As the calf hung, Dad rubbed its nose, breaking the film covering it, and swept its mouth with a finger so the uterine fluid would drain from its throat and nostrils. The calf was small, and with one more push it spilled from its mother like a soaked towel onto the fresh straw below. We rubbed the calf's chest to encourage its breathing and then hastily pulled it below its anxious mother's nose. Pushing her nose against her newborn's wet and slimy coat, she sniffed cautiously, familiarizing herself with the scent. Once confident the helpless creature before her was indeed her flesh and blood, she began quietly mooing and licking the calf clean with long, loving strokes of her tongue.

I winked at Kristin as she continued to cower behind the fence and thanked her for her help. Smiling, she promised that next time we could stay in the house with our feet up and she would happily handle the task herself.

The calf was not yet standing and appeared weak. It was important that it found its mother's udder and have some milk before we left it for the evening, so I approached the young animal and gently began to coax it up onto its wobbly legs. It is then that I noticed the poor creature had a three-foot long, pasty, blueish-grey intestine protruding from its navel.

Having never encountered such a thing and unsure of our options, Dad dispatched me to the house to call the vet. I returned ten minutes later with gun in hand. The conversation had been brief. The vet advised that the navel was the last part of the calf to mature during gestation and, from time to time, it did not seal prior to birth. If the intestine had been exposed to an unsanitary environment, such as a barn floor, it was contaminated and there was nothing (barring significant, expensive, and unfeasible medical intervention) that could be done. An infection would follow and the calf would be dead within a few short and uncomfortable days.

The only humane option was to save the calf from the misery of a slow, painful death and end its life as quickly as it had begun. Without hesitation, and with Kristin covering her ears, I carried the calf out of the barn, laid it on a soft pile of straw, and ended its life.

Black Sam and Dino (Dino not yet full-grown)

CHAPTER 11
DINO'S ADVENTURE

I was in my late teens before Dad purchased our first cattle trailer. Before that, cattle were transported on the back of our half-ton Mercury pickup Dad had bought new in 1968. It was the one and only new truck Dad bought in over fifty years of farming. Dad always smiled when he talked of returning home as a young man with a gleaming new truck. It was solid and dependable, and hauled, pulled, and transported all manner of things for over thirty years before finally being sold.

The truck was modified for the task by inserting wooden cattle racks into the three anchor holes situated on the top lip along each side of the truck box. The cattle racks were, in essence, small, portable fences four feet high with two-by-fours acting as the posts and rough one-by-fours making up the horizontal planks, all of which were painted bright red to match the truck. The posts were shaved down just enough so that they fit snugly into the box holes. Once jammed into place, it took considerable strength to yank them free. Further barricades were fitted to the front and back and lashed together with a series of chains and steel rods, making a secure box capable of transporting three or four yearlings. In the winter, a heavy tarp was draped over the front and top of the racks to break the wind, and the truck bed was lined with a thick layer of fresh straw to provide some comfort in the biting cold.

For larger loads of up to twelve animals, the 1964 International three-ton grain truck was used. As with the pickup truck, cattle racks were fastened to the sides, front, and back to provide the required security, and the middle section of the end gate was replaced with a sliding door crafted from three-quarter-inch plywood that was slipped into place behind the rump of the last animal squeezed aboard. The objective was always to pack as many animals into each load as was physically possible. Partly for the economies of scale, as it was more cost-effective to travel to the city with a full load, but mostly it was done out of necessity because, if the cattle were given any room to shuffle, they would. Thousand-pound animals nervously shifting their weight on the back of a rickety old grain truck as it speeds down the highway creates unnecessary stress for all involved.

Typically, our cattle were taken to market in either Prince Albert or Saskatoon. As Prince Albert was considerably closer, it was always our first choice. I used to love accompanying Dad on those trips. We never said much on the drive in, counting the miles as they crept past and praying the truck would make it without incident and that none of the cattle would go down.

Once there, we would back into place and let out a sigh of relief as the confused cattle were shooed from the truck and herded down the slippery ramp and into a waiting holding pen to await auction. After Dad signed off on the manifest confirming the contents of the load, we would walk along the old, narrow wooden bridge constructed high above the dozens of square pens and look down on the sea of milling, mooing animals beneath us. We would scan the pens, looking for our cattle, and once found would stop and lean over the railing, watching them with pride for a moment before turning our backs and walking away. I remember the pungent smell of fresh manure, mud, and saliva coupled with the constant distraction of cattle bawling and banging while men yelled orders and trucks roared in and out in a constant stream.

At times, often on the rumour of higher prices, Dad would take a load of cattle to Saskatoon. Given Saskatoon was over two hours drive each way, we hauled there sparingly. On one such trip, it was decided Dino would go. Dino was a big, beautiful Hereford bull purchased four years earlier from Parkvista Hereford Farm in nearby Parkside. He was a giant, standing five feet tall at the shoulders and weighing in at twenty-four hundred pounds. His horns were the size of a man's arm and wrapped perfectly around his enormous head in a sweeping C, meeting at the middle of his forehead. He walked tall and proud and was an intimidating sight as he lumbered confidently across the pasture.

The other bull on the farm at the time was a homegrown Angus Hereford mix named Black Sam. Black Sam was squat and powerful with a jet-black coat excepting a shock of white fur that jumped from his forehead. He was not as big as Dino and lacked horns, but was equally fearless and cocky. The two were fast friends during the winter, but come summer when it was time to compete for the affection of females, it was a different story. For the most part, the two kept their distance when the cows were in heat, sticking to their respective herds. When fate happened to bring them together, their meetings were rarely cordial.

It was frightening and fantastic to see them fight. I remember watching, wide-eyed in awe while my stomach fluttered with fear and excitement, as the two creatures recklessly threw themselves into each other, trying desperately to maim their opponent. Four tons of flesh, bone, and muscle repeatedly and deliberately crashing together with ill intent has a sickening sound that scrunches your face and tightens your neck as you instinctively cringe.

They would fight for hours until exhaustion or injury forced surrender. In the process, they would carve out a path of destruction as they tore up the ground and threw each other through fences like a bowling ball through matchsticks. Planks, posts, and wire all snapped helplessly in their wake. I have a clear memory of Dino tossing Black Sam against a power pole and seeing the pole bend and vibrate from the force of the blow.

The fights infuriated Dad. The bulls could literally kill each other; however, at that point, their safety was typically not his primary concern. It was the disrespect these animals showed to the fences Dad had painstakingly constructed that drove him mad. Dad rarely got upset. His patience and control were two of his virtues. Each man has his breaking point, however, and bulls fighting was one of Dad's.

When he noticed them fighting, Dad would run up to the house and grab a baseball bat and rush out to meet the bulls where they battled. He would jump into the fray and indiscriminately club them over the head with the bat with all of his strength while yelling at them to "get the hell outta here!!"

A fight between two crazy males became a fight among three. It was terrifying to watch, and I prayed for Dad's safety and looked for a bigger stick to replace the bat when it inevitably broke. His tactics did have some success; even an animal as big and powerful as a bull feels the sting of a bat swung by a fit man with all of his strength.

Despite Dino's behaviour around Black Sam during mating

season, he was otherwise very well behaved. He had been a show bull as a yearling and was still quite tame and comfortable around people. Dad used to like to show off for family and friends by jumping onto Dino's back and scratching him with a garden rake kept by the bull pen for that purpose as Dino rocked on his legs, wagged his tail, and snorted his approval.

After four years on the farm, Dino's time had come. To ensure the bloodline of the herd remained pure, no bull was ever kept more than three or four years. Calves Dino had sired were now entering the herd as replacement heifers, marking the end of his stay. So Dino was loaded onto the International Loadstar together with as many old cows as could be packed in around him. His head could be seen above the racks, sniffing the air as the truck pulled out of the yard bound for Saskatoon with Dad at the wheel and Mom along for the ride.

The trip in was uneventful as the animals calmly enjoyed the ride. Regardless, Mom and Dad let out a sigh of relief as they pulled into the slaughterhouse and unloaded the unsuspecting animals.

As Dino stepped from the truck, the attendant recording the deliveries stopped in his tracks as he watched Dino pass. He yelled to Dad, "Sir, we can't take that animal. He's too big."

"Too big?" Dad asked.

"Way too big; he won't fit our rails. We can't take 'em bigger than nineteen hundred pounds" was the reply.

"What am I supposed to do with him?"

"I don't know, sir, but he can't stay here. You have to load him up. You could try the packing house across town."

Dino was directed reluctantly back onto the now-empty truck while Mom and Dad hurriedly took directions to the slaughterhouse situated on the other side of the city.

With Mom frantically yelling directions, Dad pushed that big old green truck through the unfamiliar city streets while Dino paced anxiously from side to side within his now-spacious cage. With his nostrils flared and his head held high, Dino peered over the sides and grunted in discontent as he tried to make sense of his situation and evaluate his options. The truck awkwardly lurched and swayed, mimicking Dino's movements as Dad forced the vehicle toward their new destination before it closed for the day.

With immense relief and a nervous smile, they located the second slaughterhouse and raced through the entrance as their eyes frantically scanned the premises for any sign of life. Anxiously, they drove up and down the length of the complex, searching for an unloading dock or an attendant. Unable to find either, they concluded the premises must be closed. The knots tightened in their stomachs. This was not good. Dino would have to come home.

Having resolved that there was no other choice, and desperately wanting to get as far out of the city as possible before nightfall, Dad pulled on the big steering wheel and pointed the truck toward the freeway leading to the road home.

Dino could sense their concern, which caused his own stress level to rise. With each passing minute, he became more agitated as he shuffled his weight from side to side and flung his huge head over the side, glaring left and right as he searched for an escape.

"He's gonna jump," Dad declared, realizing the inevitable, and he floored the truck and raced toward home, hoping speed would dissuade Dino from trying anything so reckless. Dad blew through red lights, leaning on the horn and causing Mom to take a short break from her now continuous prayer to scream through her open window, "Coming through, coming through, we've got a bull, we've got a bull!"

Then, when mere minutes from the highway, the ever-increasing traffic and a red light in the distance forced Dad to slow the truck to a crawl as unsuspecting cars surrounded them. Sensing his opportunity, Dino took a step back and threw himself over the left side of the truck, taking a five-foot section of the side with him as the cattle racks cracked and snapped under his weight. Dad watched in disbelief and horror as his side view mirror filled with the image of the massive beast clearing the side of the truck, not to mention an adjacent lane filled with cars, and landing upright and dazed in the adjacent ditch.

Dad immediately leaned on the horn and wrestled the truck to the side of the road as Mom went white and prayed harder. Slamming the truck into park, Dad leapt from the truck and defiantly marched toward Dino with his fists clenched with rage while cars filled with wide-eyed, disbelieving passengers slowly filed by, trying to make sense of the strange sight before them.

As Dad approached Dino, he slowed, stretched out his arm, and with a calm and steady voice reassured the bull that everything was alright. Likely stunned from the impact of his jump and the confusion that surrounded him, Dino stood still and let his old friend approach. Dad grabbed onto Dino's nose ring that remained intact, having never been removed from his days in the show ring. Letting out a sigh of relief, Dad stood on the side of the freeway in the heart of a city of two hundred thousand people with a twenty-four-hundred-pound bull at the end of his grasp and contemplated his next move.

With a major shopping centre as his backdrop, Dad handed Dino over to Mom as he raced back to the truck and manoeuvred the vehicle back against a nearby landscaping berm bordering the shopping mall. Dad then raised the box, bringing the back end flush with the ground, and removed the end gate. The plan was to lead Dino right back onto the truck, secure him to the side, and try again.

Hurrying back to where Mom was reassuring the restless Dino, Dad took Dino by his nose ring and began to patiently lead him the fifty metres to the waiting truck.

As Dad and Dino began their unlikely walk, an impressed little boy no more than eight years old emerged from nowhere and skipped alongside Dad, striking up a conversation.

"Hey mister, whatcha gonna do with that bull?" he asked innocently.

"I'm taking him home," Dad answered.

"That sure is a big bull, mister."

"Yes, yes he is," Dad replied with a chuckle.

As Dad continued his march with the bull and the boy, a police officer pulled onto the scene and reluctantly approached the motley bunch.

"Sir, you can't have that bull here," he astutely commented.

"Yes, thanks, we understand that," Dad replied. "Believe me, sir, it is not by choice that I am leading a huge bull by its nose along a busy freeway in the middle of the city."

Blushing, the officer listened to an explanation of the preceding events before heading to his car to call the slaughterhouse in hopes of determining if in fact there was someone available to accept the animal. There was. In their panic, Mom and Dad had failed to notice the open unloading dock on the far side of the complex.

As Dad tied Dino to the intact side of the truck box with some salvaged rope, Mom collected the splintered boards and tossed them into the truck. With Dino back where he belonged and their heart rates slowly returning to normal, they pulled onto the road and headed back toward the slaughterhouse with the benefit of knowing exactly where they needed to go.

They found the unloading dock and, with immense relief, watched Dino trot off the truck into a secure holding pen. With a slight smile breaking the corner of his mouth, Dad nodded a quick goodbye, hopped back behind the wheel, and started home.

Me with one of my calves, 1986

CHAPTER 12
MAKING MONEY

Being an ambitious sort, I was always looking for an opportunity to make a dollar. My first paying job, at the age of six, was selling gophers I had trapped in our pasture to Mr. Hien, the high school biology teacher, to feed the classroom snake. I was paid twenty-five cents apiece. I remember the feel of the coins in my hand after completing my first sale and the swell of excitement and possibility that filled my belly as I imagined the untold wealth that the arrangement could bring. Unfortunately the snake in question only ate once a month, so despite my willingness to hunt down every gopher within a ten-mile radius of the farm, my first introduction to capitalism wasn't particularly lucrative.

Picking bottles was another favourite moneymaker. Beer bottles would fetch five cents each and large glass pop bottles as much as twenty-five cents. I was completely bewildered as to why anyone would toss a bottle out the window of their car. Did they not know all you had to do was take the empty bottle back to the store and you would be paid? Could they not read the label? Did "Return for Refund" mean nothing to these people?

As a young boy I would walk the ditches for miles in each direction from our farm, searching for bottles. The trick was convincing my sisters that the exercise was worth their time as well, as it greatly increased my efficiency if I could persuade Heather, Colleen, and Erin to walk the ditches while I couriered the loot back home on my bike in continuous shuttles. Colleen and Erin were usually an easy sell; Heather, not so much, as she appeared immune to my natural charm and the lure of great wealth. She generally required a side deal of some sort before agreeing to participate.

If successful with my pleas, the girls would walk the ditches as I would bike slowly ahead, encouraging them to look carefully and move faster. When a dozen or so bottles had been found and divided equally between two plastic bags, I would slip the handles of one bag up each arm, excitedly hop onto my bike, and pedal furiously back home. I took the task much too seriously not to rush. Time was money after all.

After carefully lining up the bottles by category: beer bottles, pop bottles, big pop bottles, and others, I would climb back onto my bike and race back, eager to report the current status of our growing inventory and hoping the girls had found so many bottles in my absence that I would be forced to turn right back around without rest.

If we were lucky enough to find even a few dollars' worth of bottles to show for an afternoon of work, I would declare the venture a huge success and immediately begin planning for the next search.

On the next trip to town, one or more of us would accompany Mom with the bottles carefully and securely packed within a cardboard box. We would lug the bottles into our town's only convenience store and plunk them upon the counter to be counted. I would count along silently in my head, ensuring every nickel that was owed to us was included in the tally. When the math was complete, the till would pop open with a ring and the coins and a few small bills would be dropped into my eager hands before being split with my sisters. Sometimes a small candy or two was purchased from the profits, but generally I simply deposited the money into my piggy bank with plans of bigger and better things.

When I was fourteen, I spent the entire winter cutting wood in my spare time. Our hired man, Delbert, had inspired me. When he wasn't working for Dad or engaging in one of his many varied vocations, he cut, bucked, and split white poplar, birch, jack pine, and spruce in the surrounding forests for firewood. He would haul the wood home in ten-foot lengths and buck it into eighteen-inch pieces in the yard. The pieces would then be split by a homemade splitter, which consisted of a large, salvaged flywheel (several feet in diameter) to which an axe-head had been welded. A belt stretched out from a pulley on the side of the flywheel and connected to a small gas motor that rotated the wheel in an endless cycle. A log would be placed in its path as the axe-head passed through a crudely fashioned gap in a thick steel plate affixed to the front of the contraption. If all went accordingly to plan, the axe would slice through the log with little fanfare as the momentum of the blade split the wood.

In an endless cycle, Delbert would retrieve a log from the pile, rest it against the plate with his hands cupping the sides, and wait for the blade. *Crack.* One piece would become two, and with a single, fluid motion, the resulting firewood would be tossed onto a pile to dry. Depending on the wood, Delbert was paid forty to sixty dollars a cord. Despite the fact that a cord is a tightly packed pile four feet wide, four feet deep, and eight feet long, this seemed like a fortune to me and much too good of an opportunity to pass up. So, for an entire winter on any day where we finished chores while there was still some light in the sky, I grabbed a chainsaw and a tattered old packsack filled with gas, oil, and tools, and hurriedly trudged a half mile through the deep snow to a fifteen-acre pocket of white poplar growing in the middle of the home section.

Once there, I would fire up the saw and begin felling trees as quickly as I could safely do so. Scanning the forest, I would search out the biggest, tallest trees. Once a tree was selected, I would study its stance, looking for signs of a natural lean, a bow in the trunk, or lopsided branches that would influence its direction of travel once cut. I also had to consider the most logical spot to drop the tree and whether the path of travel was blocked by dead, brittle branches that could snap under the weight of the tree as it crashed by, flinging limbs unpredictably in all directions.

When comfortable with my decisions, I would cut a notch a third of the way through the diameter of the trunk slightly above the snow line on the side of the tree facing the direction I wanted it to fall. I would then manoeuvre the saw to the other side and begin another cut several inches above the notch at a fifteen-degree downward angle. The objective was to force the tree to buckle toward the side weakened by the notch as the blade fought its way through the fresh wood.

As the blade reached the halfway mark, the tree would begin to lean, the whine of the saw echoing off the trees and the smell of gas and oil filling the air. Squinting through the sawdust while my heart pounded with anticipation, I would hold the throttle open and force the blade against the wood while listening for the familiar *crack* as the trunk snapped under its own weight and came crashing to the forest floor.

As soon as the tree hit the ground, I would work up from the base, lopping off branches until I had reached the far end where I would turn around and toil back, bucking the tree into eighteen-inch lengths. When several trees had been cut, limbed, and bucked, and the chain on the saw began to droop and run dry, I would shut the machine down and slog through the snow and underbrush, collecting and piling the freshly cut wood.

I worked like a dog in the cold and snow, wrestling with the saw and branches as sweat soaked my clothes. I loved that it was hard, that it made my muscles ache, that I could see the piles of wood grow with each trip.

As the last of the afternoon sun slipped past the tree line, I would gather up my gear and begin the long walk home alone through the forest and across the barren fields, guided by the glow of the yard lights in the distance.

I cut three cords that winter. I loaded it all up the next fall on the hay wagon and brought it into the yard where it created one modest pile beside the big shed. I never ended up selling a single stick, because we burned every bit in the woodstove in the shop. That was fine by me; I was proud of what I had accomplished and that my work had benefited the family. I didn't need to be paid to feel like the effort had been worth my time.

Livestock was the focus of many of my entrepreneurial schemes. For my twelfth birthday, I received my first cow, a black, white-faced Angus Hereford cross. When I came up for breakfast that morning, a lone card sat on my empty plate with no sign of a present. I stood at the table and curiously opened the card as my smiling parents and sisters surrounded me. Reading the inscription, I discovered much to my joy that my gift was a young heifer that had just given birth to her first calf hours earlier. That gift meant so much to me. I felt as if my hard work and dedication was being recognized and rewarded, and that I was being welcomed into manhood. Hugging my parents, I thanked them, fighting back tears, before rushing outside to the barn to check on the beginning of my herd.

I turned the corner of the barn, wide-eyed with excitement, and walked slowly up to my cow and wobbly calf, reassuring them as I went. Stopping just short, I knelt in the straw before them and watched them watch me as I grinned from ear to ear and soaked in the moment. I was so proud to tell people I had my own cattle, even if my herd consisted of a single cow and her lone calf.

That first cow turned out to be a really good animal; she never lost a calf in all the years I owned her and was always a reliable and doting mother. Her second calf was a nice heifer, so I made the decision to forego the profit I would have earned by selling and instead held on to her, expanding my herd to two. So each spring for many years to come, I had two calves to sell. It was always exciting to help Dad load my yearling for auction and wait with anticipation for the resulting cheque to arrive in the mail. Every penny of the money earned was put in the bank, allowing me to graduate high school with enough money saved to pay for the first several years of university.

A less profitable venture involved rabbits. Having easily convinced myself that rabbits would be a great way to make a nice living, I bought two rabbits from a friend when I was in fifth grade. After much negotiation, it was agreed that I would pay two dollars apiece for a male and female. The transaction was finalized in the schoolyard before the first bell. In return for four dollars, I was handed a small cardboard box, complete with two rabbits as promised. I could barely get through the day and I struggled to concentrate on my schoolwork, eager to get home and introduce the rabbits to the pen Dad and I had fashioned.

We had built an impressive home for the rabbits consisting of a warm, dry, enclosed house together with a yard, all elevated two feet above the ground on the six posts that made up the foundation. The covered enclosure was three feet by six feet with a small hole that opened up into another pen, which consisted of a wood floor twice the size of the enclosed portion, framed and wrapped in chicken wire to create an exterior cage six feet wide, six feet long, and three feet high. It was accessible by a small, sliding door affixed to the far end that was just big enough to allow me to crawl through into the pen to clean up the rabbits' nuggets as they accumulated.

The covered portion of the house also had a small, sliding door barely large enough for me to squirm through and had been stuffed with fresh yellow straw a foot thick. The exterior pen had fresh water and alfalfa picked from the ditch early that morning.

When the day finally ended, I excitedly gathered up my rabbits from the cloakroom where they had waited patiently all day and rushed to the bus for the short ride home. As the bus came to a stop outside our farm, I scurried from my seat and out the door, running down the driveway as my sisters giggled behind me. I headed straight for the rabbit pen, eager to show my new pets the fresh world that awaited them.

Carefully reaching into the box, I gently pulled each rabbit out and placed them into the outside portion of the pen. Their noses twitched as they slowly and deliberately hopped around the pen, familiarizing themselves with their new surroundings. I watched each movement with glee and wonderment, anxiously waiting for them to find the water and food I had carefully placed, and hoping they would find the opening into their home without difficulty. When they bounced with approval through the small door into the house, I ran around the back of the enclosure and quietly peered through the cracks in the roughly hewn wood, smiling as I watched them continue their exploration. With some trepidation they shyly shuffled about, sniffing the air with their noses and trembling whiskers. Soon they were right at home, confident and comfortable in their new surroundings.

Caring for the rabbits was then added to my list of daily responsibilities. I have many happy memories of picking a handful of crabapples on a hot August day and sauntering down the road, heading out of the farmyard and into the nearby ditches, searching for the biggest, freshest clumps of alfalfa and grass. I would tear out the plants at their base and carry huge armfuls back to the pen for my hungry rabbits.

The fresh food would be carefully placed and any remnants of the previous meal swept out to ensure a clean and sanitary environment. The water bowls were filled daily with fresh, cold, clean water and I often pulled leafy branches off surrounding trees and carefully placed them into the exterior pen, deliberately trying to fashion a little forest so the rabbits could nibble on the leaves, chew on the bark, and pretend they were living in the wild. I loved holding a single blade of grass in my hand and feeding my pets. They would grab at the meal and begin pulling on the blade with tiny rhythmic bites as their cheeks filled and bulged. When the opportunity presented itself, I would also feed them carrots, lettuce, or any other treat from the garden I thought they might enjoy and Mom would not miss.

I regularly cleaned the pen from top to bottom, taking great pride in ensuring the enclosure was spotless and well maintained. Old, worn, and lifeless bedding would be raked, shovelled, and swept out and replaced with fresh straw. Every twig, stalk, and dropping was swept and removed.

One day I approached the pen to carry out my daily tasks and discovered, to my complete shock, a tiny bunny sitting against the edge of the cage, staring out into the world. I could not believe my eyes as I did not know that one of the rabbits was pregnant. My heart was racing a mile a minute. I had no idea what to do and was terrified that its mother had abandoned the poor creature as the adults were huddled inside the shelter in a nest of straw.

Without thinking, I flung open the door and reached in and grabbed the frightened little creature in my hands. It was so warm, soft, and fragile it felt as if I was cupping a ball of cotton. I ran to the house, eager to share the news and receive some guidance as to where this little creature had come from. On the advice of my parents, I called Calvin Rinas, an older friend of mine whose family farmed down the road and had many rabbits.

"Calvin," I yelled excitedly into the phone, "I found a tiny bunny in the rabbit pen when I was doing chores."

I am not sure what I was expecting to hear but Calvin, who was unimpressed with my big news, simply asked, "Well, did you touch it?"

"A little bit," I lied, as the tiny bunny shivered in my hand.

"Oh geez, well then you got to kill it," he replied. "Its mother won't take it now."

I was horrified. I hung up the phone and ran back outside with the bunny held tightly against me, trying hard to keep from crying. How could I have been so stupid? I had sentenced this poor creature to death.

Despite Calvin's instructions, I could not bring myself to kill the bunny. I could not possibly believe a mother would destroy its young simply because I had made the innocent mistake of holding it. I tried desperately to think, praying for an answer to my seemingly insurmountable problem.

Finally, I concluded Calvin could not possibility be right. No mother would be so heartless. I raced back to the rabbit pen, pulled open the door, and gently climbed inside having decided

I would simply hand the baby back to its mother and pray for the best. I already knew the worst possible outcome, so there did not appear to be much to lose.

My heart raced as I manoeuvred inside the cramped quarters, crawling slowly toward the mother. As I approached, she darted past me out into the exterior, revealing, much to my joy and immense relief, three more tiny little bunnies snuggled contentedly in a warm bed of straw and fur. I could not believe my eyes. Quickly, before I could do any more damage to the delicate balance of nature, I lovingly placed the bunny back among its siblings, shimmied back out the door, and hid quietly behind the pen, peering sheepishly through a crack between the planks.

I waited and waited as the minutes crawled by. Finally, I heard the soft, hesitant patter of rabbit feet as the mother cautiously returned to her young. She peered through the doorway with ears perked, carefully surveying the room while her nose twitched suspiciously and her whiskers bounced along. After satisfying herself that I had left and the threat had passed, she hopped slowly toward her nest with an outstretched neck, searching for any lingering hint of danger. I held my breath and waited, terrified that at any moment my sin would be revealed and I would witness the ultimate parental rejection. Hop, another hop, and then finally the mother stood directly over her young, gently touching her nose to each of theirs in a quick kiss of recognition. Then, without a hint of hesitation, she cuddled among her four little bundles of fur. Calvin was wrong. I smiled, began to breathe again, and promised to think before acting in the future and to never blindly follow advice.

By the next summer, my two rabbits had become nine and I convinced Dad that more room was needed for my animals to run as they were much too cramped in their current accommodations. The rabbits were fine of course, but Dad always encouraged my ambitious schemes and set about helping me pound in the posts needed to make an addition adjacent to the existing pen.

My vision was to create an environment that mimicked a bush rabbit's natural surroundings to the greatest extent possible. With that objective in mind, we pounded in posts running out from the south side of the pen, creating an addition that was fifteen feet long and ten feet wide at it deepest point. The west side was walled in with planks running four and a half feet tall, which continued around the south side where a large door was constructed for easy access. The east side was enclosed with chicken wire with two-by-sixes creating a base and top rail. The south side, which bordered the original pen, was completed by adding boards to the existing structure to create a fully enclosed cage.

Chicken wire was then laid directly upon the ground, anchored into the bottom boards and painstakingly joined together by overlapping each piece six inches over the next and then connecting them together by wrapping short pieces of haywire between them at eight-inch intervals. This allowed the grass to grow up through the wire, but blocked any attempt by the rabbits to tunnel their way to freedom.

To add authenticity, I dug up and transported a dozen wheelbarrow loads of fresh soil from the nearby field and dumped it into one corner of the pen so the rabbits would have a place to dig and frolic. I then dragged broken logs and rocks from the nearby bushes and strategically placed them within the pen as I worked to create a replica of life in the wild.

I was immensely proud of the finished product and got great joy from watching my rabbits enjoy their new accommodations. Unfortunately, my creation had two significant design flaws.

First, I had not accounted for how compact rabbits could be if the situation called for it. On the second day after the unveiling, I walked up to the pen with fresh food in hand only to discover it was vacant. Every single rabbit was missing. I was dumfounded; how could they have possibility escaped?

A quick search of the new addition revealed that they had managed to dig out through a small gap no larger than four inches wide, beside a post that I had been unable to adequately anchor the chicken wire to. It was devastating for me.

I ran around the yard desperately looking for my rabbits, poking under grain bins and rustling through the garden. It did not take long to find them as they darted to and fro throughout the yard. It took the dogs even less time to discover them as they began to run wild with excitement, chasing any rabbit they could see under the nearest building or piece of machinery. It was clear the rabbits would not survive long if they were not returned to the safety of their home.

Dad was confident the rabbits would return to their enclosure to drink and eat despite the abundance of food and water throughout the farm. He also surmised that they would also almost certainly seek refuge from the dogs in the safety of familiar surroundings.

Counting on this behaviour, we filled the pen with fresh food and water and did our best to keep the dogs away. Dad then quickly fashioned an ingenious trap. He found a big discarded sprocket among a pile of scrap metal that fit perfectly over the freshly dug hole. The sprocket was too heavy for the rabbits to push aside when it rested against the ground, thereby blocking any entrance or exit. Several pieces of rope were then tied together and stretched nearly one hundred feet away from the pen, ending behind a clump of apples trees far from the view of any rabbit that might approach the pen. The other end of the rope was secured through the hole in the middle of the sprocket, and the sprocket was then anchored to the side of the pen with a series of fencing staples and aligned directly above the hole. With the string pulled tight and fastened to a tree at the far end, it hung a foot directly above the hole, allowing the rabbits to come and go as they pleased. When the string was released the sprocket would come crashing down, blocking the hole and trapping inside any rabbit that happened to be within the pen at that time.

With the trap set, I went about my chores, not convinced the contraption would work but desperately wanting to find out. After my chores were done, I carefully snuck back to the string and, with one quick yank on the dangling end, released the slip knot and brought the weight at the opposite end slamming down to the ground. I dashed to the cage as my heart pounded and my stomach clenched, straining my eyes and neck, desperate for a view of the cage at the earliest possible moment. As I approached, I saw a flash of fur. It worked; I had caught one! My stomach began to untangle as I let out a yelp of joy and pumped my fists in excitement.

I hopped over the fence into the pen and gently chased my prisoner into the original pen while playfully scolding it for being so foolish as to escape. With the rabbit secured, I reset the trap and ran off to tell Dad the good news.

Several times each day for the following week, I would spring the trap and then run excitedly to the pen to see if any more rabbits had been captured. Sometimes there was one or more, sometimes none, but by the end of the week each of my rabbits was back within the safety of their newly fortified home.

The second design flaw proved to be more significant and was discovered when my cousins James, Christa, and Jens came from Regina for a visit.

My cousins arrived with Auntie and Uncle and the family dog, Ticky, a beautiful husky collie cross, shortly before I returned home from school. When the school bus pulled up to our house, my sisters and I saw their van in the driveway, scurried off the bus, and ran down the lane, eager to greet our cousins.

My cousins had never seen my rabbits and I could not wait to show them off. After the pleasantries of hugs and kisses, we all tore from the house and headed straight for the rabbit pen.

"I sure hope they're outside using the new pen," I thought as we ran. I was eager to point out to them all the work I had done and explain the attention and thought I had put into each and every detail.

I got part of my wish, about half of the rabbits were outside. The only problem was they were dead. Their warm corpses were scattered throughout the various pens. There was not a single survivor.

I was in complete and utter shock. My sisters began to cry and ran back to the house faster than they had come. I stood there with James and Jens and stared, dumbfounded, into the pen while I tried to make sense of the sight before me. Questioning the truth before me, I hopped over the fence and gently nudged at each body hoping there was some other explanation. There wasn't. They were all dead.

"It must have been a hawk," I suggested, unable to comprehend any other explanation.

It was pretty clear that nothing could be done, so I found a box in a nearby granary and gathered up the bodies while fighting back tears. The three of us then walked sombrely back to the house in an impromptu funeral march as I carried the evidence to show my parents.

Into the house we stumbled and stood slouched and sad at the back entrance where my parents had gathered with Aunt and Uncle, trying to console the girls. It was too much; tears began to stream down my cheeks while I tried frantically to hide any evidence of my emotions.

"I just don't get it," I blubbered. "What could have happened?"

Glancing into the box, Uncle knew the answer instantly. He stepped out the door and yelled at the top of his lungs in a voice that made me cry harder, "TICKY, GET HERE!"

Ticky came trotting sheepishly from her refuge under a nearby tree with her tail between her legs and her head hung low. The blood on her fur erased any doubt. As she approached, Uncle reached down and grabbed her by the scuff of her neck in one powerful motion. Holding her at the end of his outstretched arm Uncle carried Ticky into the house and thrust her over the box of dead rabbits.

"Bad dog, bad dog!" he screamed before throwing her out the open door.

"How'd she get in the pen?" I asked, failing to connect the dots.

"She jumped the fence, Mark," Uncle explained.

It made no sense to me. Our dogs had never done that. There was no holding back now as my mind filled with visions of terrified rabbits running helplessly within their cage as Ticky chased them down one by one. The tears streamed down my cheeks and I tucked my chin into my chest and wiped my nose.

"How much those rabbits worth, Mark?" Uncle asked.

"I was hoping for two bucks apiece," I managed.

Uncle reached into his back pocket, pulled out his wallet, and began counting out two dollars for every rabbit in the box. As he counted, my tears began to slow. My sinuses cleared. I started feeling better and grinned ever so slightly.

When he was done counting, he said he was sorry and handed me the money. I said it was okay and that I was feeling much better.

I took the money and bought replacement rabbits. Before I put them in the cage, I found a big roll of sheep fencing and stretched out and installed piece after piece on the top of the exterior cage until a protective roof had been constructed. We never lost another rabbit.

Dad standing in front of harvested spruce, 2007

CHAPTER 13
LOGGING

With few exceptions, the lumber that makes up each barn, granary, and fence on the farm came from the thick forest that covers much of the land. Even the house was constructed primarily from the tall spruce trees that line the edges of the fields and follow the curves of the sloughs.

Depending on need, but typically every five to seven years, Dad would announce that we would be taking logs in the upcoming winter. This was exciting news for me as logging was hard, rugged work and great fun in my estimation.

After the harvest was complete, the bales were in, the fall field work done, and the cattle were settled in the yard, we would head to the bush to begin the process. If we were lucky, we would be able to start before snow, or at least much of it, blanketed the forest floor.

The first step was selecting the trees. Dad would patiently trudge through the bush, stepping over fallen logs and pushing aside branches with an idling chain saw in hand while his eyes searched the forest for the tallest, thickest, straightest trees. The decision was not made lightly, and Dad was very particular. Not once did a tree come down that wasn't ready to be harvested or that could not be used.

When confident with his decision, Dad would wave me back and wait for me to be safely tucked behind a tree, far outside of the range of any danger. Then he would hold the throttle tight against the handle and force the bar with its whipping chain against the trunk as the engine screamed and spewed thick purple smoke. The chain would spit small chunks of damp, hot wood and sawdust, blanketing Dad and everything within five feet as it eagerly chewed its way through the moist wood while the air filled with the pungent smell of burning oil and gas. As Dad wrestled with the machine and forced it through the timber, the tree would begin to lean and then come crashing to the ground in a mighty orchestra of snapping branches and cracking wood.

No sooner had the tree come to rest on the forest floor than Dad would tramp off, looking for his next selection leaving me behind to limb the tree. I would hurry over, anxious to get to work, not wanting Dad to get too far ahead of me. Starting at the base of the tree, I would work my way up the trunk as fast as I could manage, lopping off the branches until a naked log was left before me.

I was no more than ten years old the first time I helped log in the bush. I remember being given a small hatchet with a red handle and a black rubber grip. I would attack the tree, swinging and hacking at the branches as the sweat poured off me. The little branches, those smaller than the size of a finger, could be plucked off with a single swipe, and while I was never deterred or intimidated by the size of the limb, the larger branches often proved much more difficult for a ten-year-old boy. Notwithstanding that fact, I would feverishly chop away as fast and hard as my small arms would allow, regardless of the girth of the branch before me. If I fell behind, one of the men Dad always hired to help would eventually find their way over and, much to my chagrin and their amusement, would rescue me from the futility of the situation. After several weeks of work, the forest floor would be littered with fallen trees. Before freshly fallen snow could bury the timber, we would begin the process of skidding the logs to the landing. Dad would manoeuvre our littlest tractor through the narrow skidder trails, trying to bring the tractor within reach of each log. Once close enough to attach the dragging chain, I would hop from the tractor and stretch the heavy chain toward the waiting trunk. Scanning the base of the truck, I would look for some spot within the first few feet where I could force the chain underneath the log and yank it through to complete a loop. When confident I had discovered the point that would offer the best chance of anchoring the chain, I would grab the hook in my hand and begin punching it underneath the heavy log while trying to keep the cold snow from filling my mittens.

Once hooked, Dad would inch the tractor ahead, tightening the chain to ensure it would hold. If the chain failed to catch, the process would be repeated until the links found a firm grip. Once secure, the tractor, with tree in tow, would snake through the forest to the clearing where the logs were being collected and sorted into piles to wait out the winter. Dad would pull up tight to the appropriate pile and I would jump down off the tractor and hurry to release the chain. Often the chain had bit into the soft wood against the strain of the tractor while being dragged along the frozen path and had to be pounded free with a hammer or axe. After freeing the chain, I would hop back aboard the tractor and we would head back into the bush, watching for another timber to retrieve.

By spring, the landing was filled with a collection of the best trees the forest had to offer and we could begin the process of bucking the logs into appropriate sizes. Eight-, ten-, and twelve-foot lengths were the most common, but depending on need, we would always reserve some of the straightest trees to be cut into sixteen-foot lengths for gates or other special purposes. Dad always had a good idea of what we needed and would count out estimates of how many two-by-fours, two-by-sixes, two-by-eights, two-by-tens, timbers, one-by-fours, etc., were expected and would compare that to what was needed and adjust accordingly. We would tinker away at the task all summer when time could be found, and when fall arrived and the crop was in the bin, arrangements would be made to have Jack Rudolph drag his portable sawmill down the road to slice the logs into lumber.

It was quite the production. One man on a loader tractor would retrieve the logs one or two at a time and deposit them onto a rack affixed to the sawmill. A man on each end of the freshly delivered log would then muscle the timber down the rack, using a combination of brute force and logging picks, and manoeuvre the log onto the sled. The steel wheels of the sled sat upon rails and ran the length of the sawmill, much like a train on tracks. Once positioned on the sled, the log would be secured tightly in place by a series of clamps and then fed into the massive, circular blade by engaging the drive on the sled.

The blade would scream and belch sawdust as it furiously ripped into the log. When the entire length of the log had been cut, a slab would fall off. One man would catch the slab as it was discarded and toss the heavy plank onto a slab pile. Slabs were rough and crude with bark on one side; they still had a purpose as they were often used to build windbreaks for the cattle or burned in the water troughs in winter to keep the ice from forming on the water.

No sooner had the sled completed its first pass when the man operating the mill would reverse the sled, sending the log with one freshly exposed side rushing back to the men waiting at the far end of the machine. The men would hurry to undo the clamps and rotate the log onto the flat side just created from the last pass. As soon as the log was positioned and secured, the sled would once again feed the log into the roaring blade, creating another slab and another flat side. The process would continue in perfect rhythm until slabs had been cut away from all four sides, leaving a straight and true timber. The timber would then be fed through the blade like cheese through a cheese slicer, taking off perfectly uniform boards with each pass.

The size of the tree dictated the size of the resulting lumber. Small trees were used to make two-by-fours and big trees to make two-by-twelves, timbers, or whatever was called for. It was the job of the man operating the mill to ensure the best use was made of each tree for the creation of the maximum number of boards.

As the boards fell from the log, they were picked up by two men and shuttled off to be neatly stacked to dry. Four or five boards would be laid upon the ground to provide a layer of insulation from the damp earth and then a second row of boards would be tightly arranged perpendicularly to the first row until a layer was complete. Another set of four or five boards would then be positioned perpendicular to the first layer and followed by a second row stacked neatly across them. Providing for a gap between each row allowed the wind to circulate throughout the pile, drying the damp wood. The crisscross stacking would continue until a pile reached eight feet into the air and beyond the comfortable reach of the men, at which point a new pile would be started.

It was noisy, dangerous, and hard work, but also great fun. The crisp fall air would fill with the rich smell of fresh, damp spruce and a hint of diesel and oil. The surrounding poplars and shrubs that framed the clearing boasted leaves bursting with vibrant oranges, reds, and browns, providing a striking contrast against the pockets of deep green spruce scattered about. Piles of pale yellow lumber rising in perfect symmetry against drifts of sawdust provided evidence of our collective efforts. When the last log was cut and the forest sat silent, I always felt a twinge of disappointment, knowing that years would pass before the need for logging would arise again.

CHAPTER 14
THE GARDEN

Like most farm families we had a huge garden, which produced produce well beyond our needs. I never understood why it was necessary to plant enough carrots and peas to feed a family of twenty, but my mom seemed to take great pride in being able to distribute surplus vegetables to family and friends. So each spring in early May, the family would gather on a warm Saturday morning to plant the garden.

Our garden boasted neat, uniform rows of raspberries, strawberries, peas, corn, lettuce, potatoes, pumpkins, squash, tomatoes, radishes, carrots, broccoli, cauliflower, brussels sprouts, turnips, beets, beans, and cucumbers, filling nearly half an acre adjacent to the house. Planting and tending to the garden was a responsibility shared by the entire family. Even as toddlers we participated by packing the freshly seeded rows of corn and potatoes with our naked little feet. My sisters and I would shuffle up and down the rows, following one behind the other giggling and laughing as our tiny feet compressed the soil around the freshly deposited seeds. As we grew, so did our responsibilities. By the time we were in grade school, we were made to hill potatoes and weed the endless rows.

I hated weeding. Partly because it was boring, monotonous work, but mostly because I felt it was taking me away from more important and interesting tasks, such as tending to the cattle or driving the machinery. My distaste for the job was shared by my sisters and we were not shy about letting Mom know how we felt. Expressing our feelings had little to no impact, however, and we were often sent into the garden with instructions to weed until we had filled a five-gallon pail. I can assure you it takes one hell of a lot of weeds to fill a five-gallon pail.

As soon as the task was assigned, we would each race out into the garden, not because we were eager to begin but because we all wanted to lay claim to the big weeds. We would tear about the garden with the large metal pails bouncing against our legs, indiscriminately searching out the biggest, leafiest weeds that could fill our bucket as quickly as possible. We were like kids on an Easter egg hunt as we each scrambled for our share of the "big ones" while Mom directed us from an open window, ordering us to stop pushing, pick a row, and do a good job.

Whenever possible I would try to sneak away to the far edge of the garden, which bordered a field. When Mom and the girls weren't looking, I would skip over the fence and hastily grab at handfuls of the big stinkweeds bordering the edge of the crop, which had escaped the pass of the sprayer. Some stinkweeds were ten inches tall with big, bushy leaves and stalks the size of a cigar. They pulled easily from the ground and could fill a pail in record time especially if the dirt was not shaken from the thick roots. If Colleen caught me in the act, she would run crying to Mom, upset that I would break the rules and try to cheat the system. Heather, on the other hand, would simply insist that I split half the big weeds with her. Notwithstanding these antics, it would still take well over an hour to fill a pail.

Once confident the task was complete, we would drag our heavy pails over to Mom or, if she was inside preparing supper, below the kitchen window. Standing below the window, I would yell up that I was done. The window would squeak open and Mom would stare down at me and my bucket, judging the situation.

"Push down on your weeds," she would order.

Reluctantly I would carefully lean into the contents of the pail trying my best to minimize the amount of pressure actually applied.

"LEAN ON IT HARD!" she would yell. She had seen this trick before.

Frustrated, I would again push down on the weeds, compressing them into the bucket and exposing a pail that was, typically, less than three-quarters full.

"Get back to work," Mom would order, "And do NOT come back to me until the pail is FULL!"

So back out to the garden I would trudge and continue on with the task of yanking up weeds and dropping them into the bucket. When the pail was to the point where it would not have been possible to add one more solitary weed, Mom would relent and confirm we were done. Sometimes we were fortunate enough to get twenty-five cents for our efforts, but usually our reward was simply the freedom to stop crawling around in the dirt, digging up weeds.

Picking the produce was definitely much preferred to weeding, but gruelling just the same. By late summer when the garden had reached its peak, new fruit and vegetables were ripening each and every day and required our attention. Buckets of fresh peas and beans and raspberries made their way to our table every night, together with corn, carrots, potatoes, and whatever else had been harvested the hour before. What we couldn't eat was canned, pickled, or frozen as Mom spent hours each day preserving the bounty of the garden to sustain us in the winter months ahead.

The kitchen in late August was excruciatingly hot as every burner on the stove was charged with the task of boiling glass jars and blanching vegetables. The countertops and table were filled with yellows, greens, reds, and oranges as cleaned vegetables and berries sat piled high, waiting their turn in the production line. The kitchen would burst with rich smells of vinegar and dill from pickling cucumbers or the sweet, tempting smell of fresh strawberry jam cooling in jars when Mom made jam.

Warm homemade bread straight from the oven covered in butter and drenched in fresh strawberry jam is a treat worthy of kings.

There was little food on our table that was not grown or produced on the farm. We gathered eggs twice daily from our chickens and grew every variety of vegetable imaginable. We had apple trees, raspberries, and strawberries. We picked wild blueberries, saskatoon berries, and chokecherries. We butchered cattle, chickens, and pigs. We rarely ate processed foods. Whether it be tomato sauce, soup, or pizza, it was always homemade with fresh ingredients and usually washed down with multiple glasses of milk straight from the cow.

We did not necessarily have one designated milk cow. There were often one or more animals that produced more milk than their calf could consume, causing their teats to become painfully engorged and necessitating milking to release the pressure. That cow would then become our de facto milk cow. Some cows were more agreeable than others, but none were tame. As a result, the milk cow had to be corralled each night before the milking could begin.

The first step was to chase the animal into the small pen in the old log barn. This was easier said than done. Notwithstanding tail twisting and prodding with a hay fork, some cows would simply refuse to leave their calves and would stand steadfast, defiantly snorting and shaking their heads. Not to be outdone, either Dad or I would then grab her calf with one hand under the calf's neck and the other firmly gripping its tail and muscle it into the barn as its mother chased behind, glaring and threatening to charge. The poor calf would be pushed into the pen as its anxious mother ran bawling behind, taking the bait. Once the animal was in the pen, she would be shooed over toward the far side and then held securely in place with a long, thick spruce rail, which was inserted into a bracket anchored to the manger at one end and pulled tight and chained to a nearby post on the other, creating a makeshift cattle squeeze. While this contraption kept the cow from escaping, it did little to discourage kicking. In order to ensure Dad made it through the ordeal relatively unscathed, a rope was carefully looped around the cow's outside leg and then pulled back tightly and tied to a nearby post to limit the cow's ability to kick. The rope never seemed to completely eliminate kicking, however, as many a cow would test their constraints several times during the course of the milking, sometimes managing to stretch the rope enough to graze Dad or knock the milk pail over.

By the time the cow had been secured, in winter, the last of the late afternoon light would have slipped away and the yard filled with darkness. As the light from the single bulb struggled to fill the barn, Dad would sit crouched on a rusty upside-down five-gallon pail with his head leaning into the animal's hindquarters and the milk pail held firmly between his legs. Each hand would grip, pull, and squeeze in a constant, alternating rhythm, directing streams of milk into the pail until the frothing liquid reached the brim of the bucket. I would sit contentedly in the warmth of the barn, quietly curled up with the family dog, listening to the rush of milk shooting into the pail as the cold evening wind whistled outside.

When the milking was complete, the calf and its mother would be turned out into the night and Dad and I would make our way in for supper, stumbling along the frozen, snow-covered paths and following the lights of the house in the distance.

Mom would take the fresh milk and carefully pour it while still warm through a large funnel lined with a clean tea towel to filter out the bits of straw and other impurities that had found their way into the bucket. After the milk was strained, it was placed into the fridge and left overnight so that the cream could rise. By morning a thick layer of rich cream was floating upon the surface. Mom would scoop off the cream and set it aside for coffee and desserts before placing the milk on the table with orders that we must drink all we could. Typically, one cow would produce much more milk than we could reasonably consume, despite our best efforts. Wasting a single drop was not an option, so we drank multiple glasses with each meal and ate countless bowls of warm milk pudding drizzled with Rogers Golden Syrup for dessert night after night.

I remember gagging when I first drank "town milk." It tasted so suspicious and strange. I was used to knowing where my food came from, and not being able to point to the cow from which the full glass before me originated did not seem right.

Me and Bruno, 4-H show at Prince Albert exhibition grounds, 1983

CHAPTER 15
4-H

My sisters and I were members of the Wild Rose 4-H Beef Club for many years. 4-H offered an opportunity to both socialize with other farm kids and learn more about cattle and livestock management. Without question, however, our primary motivation was to make money. At year's end, immediately following the regional show in Prince Albert, each club member would lead their unsuspecting calf through the auction ring to be sold for slaughter to the highest bidder. Given the auction audience primarily consisted of local business owners eager to support their community, a 4-H calf could be expected to bring twenty to twenty-five percent more at auction than you would otherwise hope to get for the same animal at the stockyards.

It was a rather ironic exercise. For eight to ten months we would work with our calves on a daily basis, caring for them and gaining their trust to the point where we were able to lead them calmly around a ring in the middle of town and then, at the pinnacle of that relationship, they were sold just in time for barbeque season. I can honestly say that it never bothered me much at all; I never had any illusions as to where the journey would end. The same was certainly not true for some of my fellow club members as the barns were frequently filled with teary-eyed kids come auction day.

Each fall Dad would survey the herd, looking for the best calves that showed the most promise. Four steers would be selected, one for each of my sisters and me, and kept away from the rest of the herd in their own small pen. In the middle of the corral sat a little wooden granary filled with "chop," a mixture of ground barley, oats, and straw together with some combination of additional feed supplements and minerals purchased at the local Co-op stirred in for good measure. Each morning before school and upon returning home at day's end, I would scoop one to two full pails of chop for each calf from the granary and dump the feed into a nearby trough as the hungry animals pushed and fought with each other to get their fair share.

As the pen only housed four animals, it did not have its own well and pump. As a result, I also had to carry water twice daily 150 metres across the yard from the nearest well and dump it into a water bowl propped up against the fence. Six to eight five-gallon pails of water were required twice daily. As a youngster, my wrists and arms would burn as my muscles strained against the weight of the water. Gritting my teeth, I would stubbornly attempt to carry two full pails the entire length without stopping, speed walking the last few dozen steps as the heavy pails began to slip from my fingers.

The most difficult part of caring for a 4-H calf was teaching it to accept a halter and be led. We started with a young calf, fresh from a summer of running wild through the pasture, that looked upon us with great suspicion. We began the process by corralling the calves within a small pen in the corner of the barn. Once the calves were locked within the corral, my sisters and I would stand on the fence and lean into the pen over the top rail, talking to the animals and each other, allowing them to grow accustomed to our voices and the presence of people while they paced nervously and suspiciously followed our every move. Sometimes when we had little to say to them or each other, we simply left them locked up for an hour or more with a radio playing. We repeated these simple exercises many times over the course of several weeks until the calves were no longer frightened when exposed to the sights and sounds of humans.

The next step was to introduce touch. I would stretch out over the fence with a rake or a broom and scratch the back of each calf while continuing to speak to them in a steady, soothing tone. It did not take long before the calves swayed in appreciation as the rake massaged their thick skin. By this point, the calves were relatively calm in our presence and had stopped frantically pacing the perimeter of the corral searching for an escape, so I began to cautiously enter the pen with them, rake in hand, and scratch their backs without the security of the fence between us. A few more weeks and the rake was no longer needed; I could simply walk in the pen among the animals and comb their thick hair with a cattle brush and scratch behind their ears with my fingers.

By the time the spring sun had melted most of the snow, the calves were relatively gentle and it was time to begin training them to accept a halter. By show day, each calf had to be broken and willing to be safely led around a noisy ring lined with people.

Heather, Colleen, and Cousin Anita washing a 4-H calf

We again started slowly. Initially we would only bring a halter with us when visiting our calves and drape it over the fence in plain sight of the animals while we brushed their coats. Once they had grown to accept the halter as something harmless and unthreatening, we attempted to loosely place the thick rope behind their ears, letting it dangle loosely for a while before eventually properly placing the halter snugly over their head and around their mouth. Some animals took to the halter rather easily, but others snorted and shook their heads for weeks before finally accepting the foreign contraption wrapped around them. Next we would tie them to a post for an hour or more at a time several times a week until the process became routine for them.

Having accomplished the task of haltering the calves, the biggest challenge still lay ahead—teaching them to be led. It was a chore we all anticipated with dread. Until I was in my mid-teens, Dad was always the initial guinea pig as he was the only one strong enough to have any hope of containing the calves. Dad would select a calf and place the halter with the longest lead rope over its head. When Dad signalled that he was ready, I would open the barn door and Dad would brace himself, with the rope wrapped around his lower back and held tightly in each hand as the eight-hundred-pound calf rushed wildly for the exit.

The calf would burst into the bright sunlight, kicking up its heels and flailing its head, trying desperately to free itself from the stubborn weight at the end of the rope. Dad would dig in his heels and lean back against the rope with all his strength while the powerful calf pulled him around the yard. It was not always easy to tell who was leading whom.

If the calf was getting the upper hand, Dad's eyes would search for the nearest post. Then suddenly, so as to take the calf by surprise, Dad would release the tension on the rope and sprint for the post as quickly as possible to gain enough slack so that the rope could be hastily anchored. The calf, meanwhile, convinced it had just won the battle of wills, would begin to trot triumphantly away, only to be stopped dead in its tracks and jolted back to reality when it reached the end of the rope.

If, after several attempts, nothing had been accomplished but bruised knees and rope-burned hands, Dad, in his frustration, would yell at me to go get the tractor.

"So ya don't want to walk, eh?" Dad would threaten the calf. "Well, we'll see about that!"

After backing the little tractor up into the pen within a few feet of the post currently holding the stubborn calf in place, Dad would quickly tie the end of the halter to the tractor hitch and order me to put the machine in low and drive. I would put the tractor in first gear, keep the throttle low, and drive while Dad walked between the tractor and the calf, holding onto the rope in an attempt to fool the calf into believing Dad had gained superhuman strength and that future attempts to resist were futile.

Predictably, this method typically had great success as the calf quickly came to realize it could not overpower the tractor. Often a session or two was sufficient to train the animal to walk as required, and we were always careful to ensure we never hurt the calves in the process. A notable exception was Barney, a young Hereford calf belonging to my sister Colleen. Barney must have been the most stubborn animal to ever step foot on the farm. He simply refused to walk. The poor creature would lean back against the rope while the halter compressed around his mouth and dug in behind his ears. He would refuse to take a step, preferring instead to let the tractor drag him around the yard with his hooves carving a trail into the earth, taking a handful of quick steps only when the pain of the rope become unbearable.

We tried everything with poor Barney. Dad and I would twist his tail and push on his rump while Mom inched the tractor gently along. When that didn't work, we tried hitching a second calf behind the tractor with him, in hopes that a good example would help demonstrate how much easier it was to simply submit. It accomplished nothing. Then it occurred to us that perhaps Barney was simply scared of the tractor, so we hitched the bale wagon to the tractor and Barney behind the bale wagon, but he still stubbornly refused to walk. Nothing seemed to make any difference, and despite our numerous attempts, Barney would not take more than a few steps at a time and continued to fight against the halter. Helpless and confused, we did the only thing we felt we could. We continued to drag him around the yard behind the tractor, convinced that sooner or later he would have no choice but to relent.

After many frustrating sessions, Barney eventually came to realize he could not win the battle of wills and reluctantly began to accept the halter and walk when led. By that time, however, his ears were droopy and his neck muscles stretched and tender from the constant pressure of the halter. We had succeeded in breaking him; unfortunately, it was both literally and figuratively, and he never placed well as a result. Barney was an unusual case. Teaching a calf to be led was never easy, but typically it involved a lot less aggravation for both man and beast. Most of the animals grew to enjoy the attention and the extra care they were afforded as a 4-H calf, and by show day were as tame as the family dog.

As the time for the show grew near, we would halter our calves and anchor them to a post for extended periods at a time. We would carry in fresh hay for them to eat and lead them to water as required, all in hopes of preparing them for the conditions they would experience over the upcoming week as they were displayed at the local show in Shellbrook and then transported to Prince Albert for the regional competition. Many additional hours of preparation were spent leading our animals in endless circles with their heads held high as we practiced technique and worked to ensure all involved were comfortable with the task. Each calf was trained to stand on command and accept the prodding hands of a judge sweeping over their bodies, checking the layer of fat beneath the skin. If concerned their stance was not playing to their advantage, we would pull and prod at their hooves with a show cane as necessary, to lengthen and widen their frame to create long, smooth lines. Then, when we were confident the fundamentals had been mastered, we would bathe our animals.

Their thick coats were soaked with water from the garden hose and scrubbed relentlessly with bristle brushes dipped in horse soap until every inch of their bodies was covered with thick suds. We scrubbed and scrubbed, putting our weight behind the brush until the pink of their skin could be seen beneath their clean hair. Each calf had their head, together with much of their brisket, shaved short to give the illusion of a streamlined, sleek front half. By contrast, the hair on their back legs was slicked with a thick, sticky wax and then backcombed, forcing the hair to stand on end to create the illusion of a thick, heavyset rump. Baby power was sprinkled generously on white hair to make it whiter, and shoe polish was painted on hooves to make them blacker. It was quite the production. On show day, the familiar smells of the barns were overpowered by the smells of hairspray, shoe polish, and soap as everybody worked feverishly on their animal, trying to enhance the positives and diminish the negatives in hopes of gaining some advantage.

Show day was intimidating for my sisters and me as we were left with the responsibility of leading an animal more than ten times our size through a ring surrounded by spectators gawking and chattering on the safe side of the fence. We prayed desperately that our calf would not step on our toes or spook and run, dragging us along with it. Despite our prayers and best efforts, feet were bruised and animals did panic and run. On one occasion, when leading my calf back to its stall in the barn following a judging event, the slam of a nearby truck door frightened my animal. It reared up and flung its heavy frame forward, ripping the leather halter from my hands and leaving me lying dazed, dusty, and embarrassed on the gravel road while it ran frantically through the barns. Men watching nearby gave careful chase, keeping their voices low and soothing while they worked to calm the frightened animal and grab hold of his dragging halter. They were quickly able to catch the animal, and he was back in his stall, contentedly chewing his cud long before I stopped shaking.

The final event of the show, and the climax of the season, was the auction. Each calf was led through the ring while the auctioneer nattered away at the crowd, trying to coax bids. Round and round I would lead my calf, sheepishly smiling at the crowd in hopes of garnering sympathy and encouraging a hand to rise. It often occurred to me that some well-placed tears could prove valuable at that moment, but I was never a good enough actor to attempt something so bold. So, I directed my calf in circles and shared his discomfort at being the centre of attention. Within a few minutes, the gavel could be heard slamming against the auctioneer's podium.

"Where's he going, sir?" the auctioneer would question the successful bidder.

The bidder would respond and direct the calf toward the appropriate waiting truck. With that, I would lead my calf up the ramp and into the trailer identified, where a waiting handler would remove the halter and hand it back with little fanfare. I never enjoyed that moment, knowing the truth of what awaited my calf the next morning, but I accepted it as a reality of life. With a final backward glance I would walk away and head back to the auction to join my parents and watch the remainder of the sale. Sometimes I was lucky enough to be directed to take my calf back to the barn where the new owner would retrieve him the next day, following our departure. It didn't change the inevitable conclusion, but the short delay did help alleviate any sense of guilt I felt as it allowed me to leave my unsuspecting calf tied contentedly in a stall of fresh straw with a generous forkful of the best hay under its nose, rather than cramped within a cattle trailer awaiting his final destination.

We often knew the purchasers of our animals, as friends of the family would frequently attend the auction to show their support. That created an interesting dilemma when we were invited for a roast beef supper. I recall sitting politely around the table, winking at my sisters as the nervous host sheepishly carried in a beautifully cooked roast from the kitchen while trying to avoid eye contact with my sisters and me. They did not need to worry. We had two huge freezers at home filled with our own roasts, hams, and chickens. We certainly knew where hamburgers came from in my family.

CHAPTER 16
LEAFCUTTER BEES

In hopes of increasing our revenue, leafcutter bees were introduced to the farm in the mid-1980s. The small, industrious bees, about the size of a horsefly and with a similar bite, were deposited among the fields of alfalfa each summer and charged with the task of pollinating the plants so that the tiny yellow seeds could be harvested in the fall.

In May of each year, one million bee larvae (more or less) were retrieved from the twenty-gallon drums, where they had sat dormant all winter, and divided among dozens of hatching trays. The hatching trays were simple, shallow, plywood boxes approximately two feet by two feet, with snug-fitting lids that slid securely into place. The centre of the lids was cut away and replaced with a fine mesh to allow the air to circulate freely throughout the box. Approximately twenty to twenty-five thousand larvae were carefully spread evenly around each tray, resulting in a layer about two inches deep. The cocoons themselves resembled green cigarettes four to six inches long, made up of eight to twelve individual larvae compressed together and wrapped securely in carefully cut alfalfa leaves.

Once each tray had been filled and carefully arranged within the hatching house (a small, well-insulated wooden building), heaters and fans would be distributed throughout the building and carefully monitored to ensure the correct temperature was maintained over the three-week gestation period. The goal was to release the bees just as the first few diminutive blue-and-white flowers began to emerge from the growing alfalfa, so the heat was adjusted accordingly to slow down or speed up the process as required. As the third week approached, the hatching house filled with a sweet, musty smell and the buzzing chorus of thousands of freshly hatched bees bouncing against the screen lids of the hatching trays could be heard the moment you opened the door.

When confident a majority of the bees had hatched and the alfalfa was ready to sustain them, each tray was carefully loaded into the back of the half-ton truck and wrapped in tarps in preparation for the ride to the field. We would make our way slowly down the road and into the field, snaking from hut to hut to deposit the bees.

The summer home for the bees consisted of small, three-sided wooden structures with a roof fashioned from tarps. The interior walls of each hut were lined with bee boxes hung a few days previously in anticipation of the arriving bees. The bee boxes were three feet long, one foot wide, and eight inches deep, and filled with a hundred or more Styrofoam cards stacked tightly together and held firmly in place by thin strips of wood nailed to the inside edge of each wall of the box. Both sides of each card consisted of a half circle that, when compressed against the card on either side, completed a perfect round, little tunnel six inches deep. Assisted by the colourful patterns spray-painted on the exterior surface of the cards, once compiled, each bee would lay claim to a specific hole in a particular box and return to it throughout the day with pieces of leaves chewed from the alfalfa plants as it prepared to deposit its eggs. At night the bees would back themselves deep into their home, waiting for the warmth of the sun to alert them that it was time to begin another day of work.

Stopping in front of each hut, we would hop from the truck and set four or five hatching trays on the wooden floor. The lids were then slowly pulled back very carefully so as not to crush any bees wedged against the edges of the box. As each lid was pulled away, thousands of bees would rush out from the confines of the tray and swarm around us, and the air would be filled with black clouds of teeming, hungry bees. They would crawl over our flesh and buzz about our ears as they worked to make sense of their new surroundings. Once most had made their way from the trays on their own accord, Dad and I would stir the boxes in front of us with our bare hands, coaxing any remaining bees to begin the job for which they had been deposited. We were always careful to keep over fingers spread wide and to twist our hands slowly about the tray so as not to trap any bees between our fingers and encourage a sting that could have otherwise been avoided. Experience taught us that you were most definitely going to get stung; it was just a question of how many times.

We discovered that gloves, for example, were more of a hindrance than a help as the bees could easily find their way in and would began to panic and sting the moment they had trouble finding their way out. The same was true of a shirt—they would crawl unnoticed beneath your collar as you worked and resolve to fight their way out when they discovered the error of their ways. Clearly it would have made good sense to purchase gloves with tight elastic wrists, bee hats, and form-fitting coveralls designed for the task at hand, but doing so was viewed as an unnecessary extravagance that could not be justified. So, for one day each year in early June, we toughed it out with bare hands and backs and took the stings we knew we had coming with as much good humour as we could muster.

It was really quite funny at times as we yelped and jumped about, reacting to stings as we worked. On one occasion, after depositing the last of the trays, Dad, Heather, and I were on our way home with the truck windows open, trying our collective best to shoo the dozen or so bees bouncing off the inside of the windshield out of the vehicle. We were jumpy and anxious, desperate for the bees to find their way out of the truck, having already endured our share of stings for one day. As I waved my arms toward the open windows, I let out a scream as a bee stung my bare back. Heather and Dad began to chuckle nervously at my misfortune, thankful that I had been the unlucky one and not them. Within ten seconds, however, Dad let out a yelp and swatted at his arm where he had just been stung. I was the only one laughing at this point as Heather began to squirm in her seat, anticipating the inevitable. She did not have to wait long for within moments she let out a holler, bouncing up out of her seat. We laughed together as we scratched at our bites and cursed the bees while we wove our way out of the field.

Over the following week, I would return to each hut twice a day on my motorbike to gently stir the unhatched larvae sitting in the trays, hoping to encourage the stragglers from their cocoons and into the world. At the end of the week, I would dump the remnants on the ground, gather the trays, and haul them home. For the remainder of the summer, the bees basically took care of themselves.

The bees loved hot weather; the hotter it was, the harder they worked. If blessed with warm weather and plentiful rains, almost every hole in every box would be filled to the brim by the time the first hard frost arrived and killed the bees. Following that first frost, it was time to bring the boxes home. I would drive the half-ton truck from hut to hut and load the heavy boxes packed with bees onto the back of the truck. Once home, the boxes were carefully stacked back into the hatching hut to spend the following months drying before we could begin the process of dismantling the boxes to retrieve the larvae deposited within each hole.

Stripping the boxes, as we referred to it, was slow, tedious work. The first step was to remove the fragile wooden slats nailed to the inside edge of the boxes without damaging the bees, cards, box, or the slats themselves. I would wrestle with pliers and a hammer in the tight confines of the box, carefully pulling each small finishing nail and placing it into a waiting bucket. Once the slats were off and carefully laid to the side, I would divide the contents of the box equally and reach around each end of one of the halves and pull it toward me, watchful to ensure the form was maintained and the cards did not spill apart onto the floor. The load was then placed upon the stripper, a simple machine designed by two young brothers from nearby Leask. The stripper consisted of a metal deck five feet long that fed into a mechanism that looked much like a guillotine with a dull, metal blade. With one hand stretched out and pulling on the back of the cards fitted within the walls of the deck, the other would operate the lever affixed to the blade. With each pull on the lever, the blade would descend, catching a single card and forcing it down through a channel, which fit the card perfectly. Welded to the interior walls of the chute were fingers of steel, which scraped against the card as it passed, keeping it perfectly aligned while simultaneously stripping the larvae. As the blade forced the card down, the cocoons would tumble free, falling into a collection tray attached to the bottom of the implement where gravity would funnel them into a waiting bucket.

It took considerable strength to bring the blade down with enough force to break apart the cards glued together from the work of the bees. I had to be very careful, however, to make contact slowly or the cards would crumble apart from the force and plug the chute with Styrofoam and gooey larvae that would then have to be swept away before the job could continue. So with methodical rhythm, I would pull down on the lever, forcing a single card down, then push the handle back up, allowing the next card to fall in place so the process could repeat itself in an endless cycle. There were hundreds of boxes to strip and the job took countless hours to complete.

When all the cards in a box were stripped clean, I would dump any remnants of leaves or bees from the box and then reassemble the cards and slats before stacking the box to the side and grabbing another. I would continue this process as the cold bit at my bare hands and my shoulders ached under the strain until I heard Mom call for supper.

When spring arrived, a wooden trough was assembled and filled with water and bleach. Each bee box was dipped into the murky, pungent water and held beneath the surface until bubbles stopped racing to the surface, confirming that each crevice had filled with the bacteria-killing concoction. The heavy boxes were then carefully dumped and pulled up onto a plywood ramp connected to one end of the trough while the water rushed back down the slope, splashing into the trough. Once resting on the ramp, the box was left to drip-dry momentarily in the sun while the next box was gathered up and submerged into the water, and so it went until the hundreds of boxes piled before me had all been washed.

Heavy rubber gloves and coveralls helped protect my skin from the bleach, but without the benefit of a face shield, droplets of bleach would inevitably splash up onto my face regardless of how careful I was. I kept a damp towel within reach and would quickly wipe my face before the bleach had much of a chance to sting my exposed flesh. Little could be done about the powerful smell, however, and within an hour those of us working at the task were all somewhat dizzy, with burning eyes and nostrils. We never complained about the smell of the bleach, the stings we suffered, or the fact we spent all day, every day working at such a task. We just weren't conditioned that way. From my earliest memory, each of us simply got up each morning and confronted the work before us, working hard to do the best job possible. We never saw others complain about hard work and it rarely occurred to us that that was even an option.

Leafcutter bees had been part of our farming operation for approximately ten years when I left for Saskatoon to attend my first year of university. Dad's decision to get rid of the insects shortly thereafter rested, in no small part, on the fact I was no longer available to tackle the tedious task of stripping the bee boxes. Coincidently, he also purchased his first automatic square bale picker around the same time. Two of the nicest compliments I have ever received.

Me, Luke, and Dad getting ready to feed the cattle

CHAPTER 17
BLACK COW

Of all the ill-tempered, miserable animals to ever have called the farm home, "Black Cow," as she was simply called, was unquestionably the worst of the bunch. A big, powerful Angus Hereford cross, she was jet black with the exception of a striking patch of white hair that jumped off the centre of her forehead. She would strut confidently around the yard like a schoolyard bully, never missing an opportunity to glare in our direction and snort disapprovingly.

During calving, and while her calf was young, she went from unpleasant to nasty and downright dangerous. We had to be aware of her whereabouts at all times while in the cow pen, for if you lost sight of her, or more importantly her calf, and happened to wander close enough to cause her to feel threatened, she would come charging across the pen, forcing your heart into your throat and your legs into action. Despite her unfortunate disposition, Black Cow was a fixture on the farm for many years given she was a beautiful animal that consistently raised strong, healthy calves.

We were fortunate that, in all the years she was with us, only once were we forced to help her deliver a calf. Once was enough.

Knowing her time was near, Dad had been watching her all day. He noticed that she had wandered off from the herd, as cows often do when they are about to give birth, and had settled herself down behind a handful of round bales in the far corner of the yard. Dad snuck up every half an hour or so to monitor her progress, always careful to keep enough distance and avoid her line of sight so as not to cause her concern. Several hours into the process, Dad became worried. Her water had long since broken, but nothing more than the tip of the calf's hooves could be seen as Black Cow was clearly having difficulty.

We were reluctant to come to her aid, partly because we knew she would almost certainly take a run at us, but mostly because the stress of our presence could potentially cause her such anxiety that the delivery could prove even more difficult. As time passed and she continued to struggle with little progress, it become clear that if the unborn calf was to have any chance of survival, we were going to have to intervene.

After gathering up some stainless-steel chains, a bucket of warm water, and a big stick, we nervously approached Black Cow. It was evident as we grew near that she was in considerable discomfort and having great difficulty. Despite her weakened state, she somehow found her way to her feet as we approached and stared us down, daring us to be so foolish as to take another step forward. I was no more than thirteen years old at the time, but I remember it clearly, standing there in the cool spring air on the brown grass as my heart pounded in my chest, waiting for someone to make the next move.

"Mark," Dad said, "I need to get around behind her and get these chains on the calf's feet so we can pull, but in order to do that I'm going to need you to distract her. You need to head straight toward her and get her to chase you so I can sneak behind."

I must admit I failed to see the wisdom of the plan on first blush, but Dad assured me I would be able to outrun the struggling animal in her current condition and, if need be, Dad would be there to beat her off with the stick. So, I took a few nervous steps toward her as my stomach clenched and adrenaline pumped through my veins. Black Cow snorted and shook her head violently; she was breathing heavily and was clearly in a foul mood, but I didn't heed the warnings and kept inching closer bouncing on the balls of my feet until I was less than a dozen feet away. Then, in an instant, she lunged forward and tore toward me while I let out a yelp of excitement and ran the other way, anticipating the smash of her powerful head into my back. After going thirty or forty feet, the pain and discomfort of her current condition forced her to stop and stand, panting, while Dad inched closer to her backside. Sensing something was afoot, she swung around and bore down on Dad with her head lowered and her nostrils flaring. Dad darted out of the way and ran, laughing and cursing, until the sound of pounding hooves behind him stopped. And there we stood, one hundred feet apart with Black Cow between us, panting and sweating, but nowhere close to giving in.

"Do it again, Mark," Dad instructed defiantly. "She can't

chase us all day. She'll either stop running or she'll go down."

With more confidence this time, and beginning to enjoy the rush, I again approached the animal, challenging her to give chase. Again she charged at me, trying desperately to slam her head into my body while I scurried safely out of her reach. After a few seconds of running, she stopped and spun around clumsily before making a half-hearted attempt to charge Dad. She was too exhausted by this point to run much longer. Dad motioned for me to approach again, so I hurried toward her, waving my arms and calling to catch her attention. The moment she turned and lunged toward me, Dad rushed in with a chain in hand and grabbed onto one of the protruding hooves. She quickly turned, but Dad turned with her, continuing to struggle to anchor the chain while he spun. Together they circled like a dog chasing its tail while I ran to retrieve the stick from where it lay should Dad trip and need my help in fighting off the cow.

Despite the havoc, Dad somehow managed to loop the chain and then throw his weight downward. Black Cow let out a deep, sorrowful moan, stopping dead in her tracks while her hind end dipped from the strength of Dad's pull and the pain it caused. I hurried in alongside Dad and grabbed onto the chain to maintain the pressure while Dad plunged his arm into the animal, searching for the other foot, which had retracted in the excitement. He soon had it and wrestled it forward while wet goo dripped off his arm and sweat beaded on his tense face. A second chain was wrapped around the other leg and then yanked forward until both feet were extended ten inches out of Black Cow. Together we stood shoulder to shoulder, with slim chains wrapped tightly around our bare hands.

"Pull!" Dad yelled, sending us both backwards as we leaned into the chains with every bit of strength we could muster while the heels of our boots cut into the soft ground. The pale hooves slowly inched forward with each pull as we struggled to deliver the calf. After fifteen minutes, the nose finally came into sight. It was grey and pasty, confirming the calf was in distress. We pulled harder, with more urgency, desperate to save the calf.

"Push, Bossy, push!" Dad pleaded with the cow as we all worked together with a common purpose. With a moan of pain, the head finally crested and popped free. Our relief was short-lived, for the calf was showing no signs of life. Its head hung lifeless and limp from the end of its mother and its swollen tongue could be seen forcing its way past pale lips. Dad frantically plunged his fingers into the calf's mouth, sweeping away mucus to ensure an open airway. He then rubbed the calf's nose and massaged its wet face, hoping to encourage it to take a breath.

"Come on baby, come on baby," Dad repeated earnestly as he worked on the calf. Finally, the faintest snort was heard as the calf weakly shook its head, showing its displeasure with the continued aggravation.

With hope renewed, we leaned back into the chains, yelling in unison for Black Cow to push. Arching her back against the strain, and with her tongue protruding from her open mouth as she bawled, she pushed with the last of her strength. With a sudden, sloppy splash the calf popped free and landed with a thud on the ground. Without a moment's hesitation, I began fighting to remove the chains while Dad roughly rubbed the calf's chest, persuading it to breathe.

Within seconds of the calf hitting the earth, Black Cow wheeled around and swung her head wildly in our direction, showing little appreciation for our efforts. We jumped back from where we sat crouching over her newborn calf and rolled to safety before scrambling to our feet and jogging out of her reach. Standing back and breathing heavily, we watched in silence as Black Cow tenderly licked her calf clean. Her long tongue raked across her young calf as it shook its head

139

periodically and squinted its eyes against the bright sun. Once it was clean, she began to gently nudge under the calf's hindquarters, encouraging it to stand and take its first drink of milk while intermittently glaring in our general direction. We watched as the newborn struggled to stand on its wobbly legs and instinctively made it way to its mother's udder, stumbling along on its stilt-like legs. When it reached the hind, its mouth fumbled to find a teat between its mother's legs and, once found, latched on and began to suck. The calf stood and sucked hungrily, playfully punching his head into his mother's udder as milk foam bubbled from the corners of its mouth. When confident the calf was well, we gathered up the chains and pail, together with the big stick, and made our way back to the house.

That was the last year for Black Cow. Given her advancing age, Dad was not about to take the chance that she would struggle with delivery again, especially in light of what we had experienced when trying to come to her aid. So, later that fall when the cattle came in from the pasture and her calf was weaned, we loaded her into the trailer and hauled her to market. Defiant to the end, she stood tall in the trailer as she was driven off the yard with her nose thrust out through the opening in the steel walls, no doubt plotting her escape.

Hauling square bales with Delbert

CHAPTER 18
DELBERT

From my earliest memories, Delbert was a fixture on our farm. During seeding and through the harvest, he spent more time with our family than his own and, in many ways, became a bigger part of ours. When needed, he came. He would drop whatever he happened to be doing and literally race to our farm as soon as he received the call. I can remember listening for the sound of the exhaust as the engine strained against Delbert's heavy foot and watching his pickup truck fishtail down the driveway as he made the turn off the highway. I would stand wincing while I watched the drama unfold and pray my pets and sisters were out of harm's way. My sisters managed to make it through their childhood unscathed but, unfortunately, the same cannot be said about more than one dog. Screeching to a stop in front of the machine shop where we stood waiting, Delbert would jump enthusiastically from the cab, slam the door and, while pulling up his pants and adjusting his suspenders, he would give Dad one of his "betcha never thought I could get here that fast" looks as he cocked his head and grinned from ear to ear. Often he would come right out and say it while slapping Dad on the back, not wanting to risk having anyone miss the obvious.

Dad always scolded him for driving too fast. Delbert would listen as he stared at the ground, but it was only a matter of time before the lesson was forgotten for, while Delbert was a man of many unique talents, he did have certain shortcomings. So while he could stack square bales in perfectly uniform rows upon a wagon so precisely that his loads never shifted or tumbled, back up a full grain truck to a waiting auger in a single confident pass, and remember exactly where to find a wrench hidden among endless tools in the shed, he could also have difficulty grasping certain concepts and understanding social norms and behaviours. When Delbert first came to work for Dad, he was approaching his sixteenth birthday and was in the sixth grade. When his birthday arrived, Delbert left school and never returned.

In the early years, before he received his driver's licence, Delbert would bike out to the farm to follow Dad around the yard, helping however he could. His disability made him difficult to understand when he was young and that, together with his hyper, impulsive nature initially limited his usefulness around the farm, but Dad was patient. He spent many hours with young Delbert, teaching him to how to operate machinery, care for cattle, and undertake the many varied duties that arose each day on the farm. Delbert thrived under Dad's tutelage and as the years passed and Delbert matured and learned, he became an integral part of our farming operation and a familiar face at the dinner table. His appetite was legendary and his manners impeccable. He would fill his plate high, to the point of over-flowing, before crouching over the food and hurriedly forking every morsel into his mouth. Occasionally he would comment on the events of the day but was always respectful of our family's conversations and rarely interjected. At the end of every meal, he would thank Mom for her efforts before pushing away from the table and heading back out to the yard.

Delbert was always enthusiastic about the task at hand, whether it be fencing, hauling bales, or branding calves. He never tired of the work and eagerly anticipated each day. Hauling bales was always a favourite; it was gruelling work, but Delbert relished the opportunity to exceed Dad's expectations. He would tease Dad from his perch upon the bale wagon as Dad darted about the field with the loader tractor, scooping up stooks of bales and depositing them on the wagon for Delbert and me to arrange into rows and layers as we moulded the pile toward the sky.

"Come on, Kurt, is that as fast as you can go!" Delbert would yell, giddy with excitement.

Dad would smile silently and gun the tractor toward another stook as Delbert and I worked furiously to place the bales before Dad returned with another load. The sweat would pour off Delbert as he worked, soaking his cap and the thin hair beneath. Those years, when snow covered the ground before the last loads were brought in from the fields, icicles would form on Delbert's sideburns and steam would billow up from his balding head when he removed his wet hat to sweep the sweat from his brow. The heavier the bales, the colder the air, and the harder it was, the more Delbert loved it. He would grunt loudly under the strain with great theatrics as he tossed the bales about the wagon, placing them in a specific, consistent pattern. If I happened to inadvertently place a bale out of sequence, I would be sure to hear about it, likely for hours, as Delbert would playfully tease me for my forgetfulness and proudly point out how his quick thinking in correcting my mistake had salvaged the load from certain disaster. After the last bale was placed, Delbert would be lowered from the top of the load in the tractor's outstretched bucket, grinning so wide you would have thought some great fortune had just befallen him.

He always wanted to push the limits, squeeze one last bale on the wagon, one more calf in the trailer. He got such joy from the simplest of victories. Dad often had to interject as the voice of reason, fearful an axle would snap or a calf would suffocate, and while Dad certainly experienced his frustrations with Delbert, he always treated him with respect and as a friend, and Delbert loved him for that.

With no children, nieces, or nephews of his own, my sisters and I were important to Delbert and he would never forget our birthdays. Sure as the sun would rise, he would track me down on the day, smiling and teasing as he poked at my ribs and ruffled my hair. With his eyes dancing with excitement, Delbert would bellow:

"So, it's your birthday, hey Mark!"

I would smile in acknowledgement as Delbert pulled out his oversized wallet from the back pocket of his well-worn jeans. The chain that securely anchored the wallet to his belt would jingle by his side as he turned slyly to avoid my eyes. Popping open the change purse, Delbert was always careful to let the anticipation build as the coins rattled under his fingertips. He would then select a few small coins before returning the wallet to his pocket and spinning around with his tightly clenched fists thrust out below my nose.

"Which one?" he would ask.

I would smile and tap a fist, which, if empty, would be immediately revealed while he laughed and teased some more. If I happened to guess correctly, his smile would fade momentarily and his hands would disappear behind him again before being placed in front of me once more with directions that I try again. After several rounds he would finally open his hands and drop a few coins into my hands with sincere wishes of a happy birthday. It was the same exercise for my sisters. He never missed a birthday.

I can remember combining barley late into the night while Delbert hauled the grain. Hating the solitude of an empty truck, he would hop into the cab of the combine with me while waiting for the truck to fill. The night was so black and the darkness so complete that it felt as if the whole world existed inside that cramped, hot, dusty space. Crouching on the floor beside me, he would begin to yell over the roar of the machine, telling me of his life while I listened. He told me of his friends and his family and of his hopes and dreams. But what I remember most is Delbert telling the story of meeting the woman who would become his wife. From the glow of the instrument panel, I could make out the smile upon his face as he spoke. He told of their first meeting and their courtship in a simple, direct way, but with no less meaning than others from whom I have heard similar tales. It was clear that he loved her and that there was no less value to that love. I remember feeling surprised by the story and then somewhat embarrassed for feeling that way. I had assumed, without really giving it any thought, that his feelings must be somewhat muted, or less pronounced, than my own. I was wrong, and that was an important lesson to learn.

Delbert loved to embellish stories and relished attention. I recall shooting gophers in the pasture on a hot Sunday afternoon in August with a good friend of mine after I had already left home. We had been sneaking about the pasture for about an hour or so by the time Delbert arrived and had shot a half dozen gophers at best as the small rodents were staying deep within their burrows that day. Delbert was excited to see us and was soon walking along beside us with his own rifle, consistently (and suspiciously) noticing gophers just mere seconds before they disappeared into their burrows and we were able to spot them.

After twenty minutes or so, we said our goodbyes and went our separate ways, leaving Delbert alone in the pasture to try his luck. By the time I arrived home later that day, the phone messages revealed that Delbert had called eight times at ten-minute intervals. I knew why and knew he would call again. Soon the phone rang again, and I picked it up.

"Mark, it's Delbert. You shouldn't have left, Mark, you shouldn't have left," Delbert announced, rushing his words with obvious excitement.

"You should have seen the gophers, they were everywhere! I must have shot at least twenty-five in half an hour. Oh, I bet it was more than that, yes, it was more than that; I just stopped counting."

I played along and expressed my amazement and congratulations. He somehow always managed to shoot the most gophers, find the greatest stash of empty bottles, or achieve the most unlikely of accomplishments. Luck followed him, or at least that is how he saw it.

There is something to learn from everyone and something to be gained from the most unlikely of places. Delbert taught me the importance of patience, and that worth cannot necessarily be determined at a glance but is often something that has to be uncovered. He reminds us that happiness is often a state of mind, a decision more than something to be attained. For almost forty years, Delbert made his way to our farm to help in whatever way he was asked. He was always content, always smiling, and always happy to be helping.

Tree planting outside of Ft. St. John, 1993

CHAPTER 19
TREE PLANTING

As my first year of study at the University of Saskatchewan came to an end, I decided to spend the summer planting trees in Northern British Columbia. I wanted to go tree planting for two main reasons. Firstly, I had been told that it was by far the highest-paying summer job a student could hope to obtain and, given I was responsible for my own tuition and living cost, I needed to secure employment that would pay more than what I could hope to earn on the farm. Secondly, because I had heard countless stories about how hard it was.

Long hours in gruelling conditions, sleeping in a tent, fighting off bears and bugs. What's not to like?

I knew I could do it. I was accustomed to hard physical work—stacking bales, chopping wood, wrestling calves—these were not things that scared me. By the age of six, I was out of bed and outside before the sun was up, responsible for tending both the rabbits and chickens before boarding the bus for school. By age nine, I also had the added task of feeding and watering the 4-H calves. Even on the coldest winter days, I would wake before breakfast, bundle up, and head outside into the snow and darkness. I would trudge to the well, filling two five-gallon steel pails with as much water as I could physically manage before sloshing across the frozen path to the calf pen. The heavy pails would bounce against my legs as I quickly shuffled along, trying desperately to make it as far as possible before reluctantly stopping to adjust my grip and momentarily rest my arms and shoulders.

It always took several trips to fill the twenty-gallon watering bowl while the young calves pushed and jostled with one another, eager to be the first to drink and anxious to defeat my goal of filling the bowl. I remember coming back into the house after multiple trips with arms like rubber and snow pants so frozen they would stand erect on their own before the ice melted and they crumpled to the floor. It could be minus forty with wind howling and snow blinding and I still tended to the task without complaint. Dad never offered to help and I would not have wanted his assistance in any event. Even as I child, I understood the difference between hard and impossible.

Having decided that I was going to be a tree planter, I began to consider my options. Fortunately for me, my sister Heather happened to know of someone who was putting together a crew.

I met with Cliff at a nearby McDonald's for an interview. If the truth be told, it was not so much of an interview as it was an attempt to scare me. He told stories of rookies quitting after an hour and grown men in tears as relentless flies and mosquitoes feasted on their skin. He reminisced of heavy mud and steep mountains and described the snow, the rain, the heat, and the misery I was sure to endure. Cliff spoke of blackened toenails and tendonitis, beaver fever and battered hands while he studied my reaction and contemplated whether I had the right mix of mental and physical toughness to survive.

He was clear that, given his compensation was directly determined by the number of good trees his crew planted each day, there was only a job for me if I was confident I could succeed. He did not want to waste his time dragging some rookie halfway across the prairies only to find them begging for a bus ticket home.

I assured him that tree planting was well within my skill set, and I was hired, along with my good friend Vern.

We spent the next month studying for our term finals at university and slowly collecting the list of necessary supplies.

We soon had a tent, complete with cots and sleeping bags, erected in the middle of our cramped apartment where we spent many hours studying and imagining the great adventure that lay ahead.

In the early morning hours of a cold day in early May, Vern and I piled our gear and ourselves into his old boat of a car and began the twelve-hour drive to Prince George, British Columbia, to meet Cliff and the rest of the crew he had assembled at Tawa headquarters.

While supremely confident we could handle the rigours of the job, we were both nervous as we pulled into the muddy and stark Tawa compound. Worldly we were not, and this was a long, long way from home.

There was little more than a small makeshift office perched upon temporary foundations and a smattering of sheds and garages filled with quads and trucks, shovels, tarps, and bags. Dirty, unkempt planters and foremen shuffled around, seemingly without purpose, as they awaited orders as to what contracts they had been assigned and where they would be heading to establish their home for the next three to six weeks. No one seemed concerned about our arrival, for as unproven rookies, we had not yet earned that privilege. Our clean clothes and wide eyes had betrayed us.

With no direction and no clue, we wandered sheepishly about, looking for Cliff before reluctantly making our way into the office to announce our arrival and seek instruction as to our next steps. We were curtly pointed in the direction of Cliff and soon found him in a far-off corner of the yard with several members of our crew quickly loading shovels and supplies into the back of a large four-wheel drive crew cab truck.

The introductions were short and without formality as the work continued. We immediately pitched in and began working feverishly, anxious to quickly establish ourselves as contributing members of the team. We saw ourselves as stoic, hardworking farm boys and had no intention of letting opinions to the contrary take root.

It was all new and rather confusing. There was no orientation, no crisp agenda setting forth the specifics of what lay ahead. We were all expected to fulfill the orders as they were barked and to keep our mouths shut. As I came to learn in the years that followed, careful organization and predictability are not trademarks of the job.

Within a few hours, we had gathered the crew, our orders, and our gear. I had two new shovels and clean, stiff leather planting bags complete with three large pockets and the pull string inserts designed to keep the seedlings cool and dark while they awaited their turn to be inserted into the mountain-side. New, bright, thick orange rubber boots with heavy steel toes and sharp metal spikes together with unattractive and poor-fitting cotton gloves with webs of rubber ridges rounded out my essential gear. I was now indebted to my new employer for several hundred dollars before I had even planted a single tree. Awesome.

It was mid-afternoon before our caravan was finally fully assembled and en route. We had been assigned a contract less than two hours out of Prince George, and it was essential that we arrive before the sun set, lest the task of setting up camp be unnecessarily complicated by the lack of light.

We were quite the collection of misfits. There were bible school students and former convicts, an old "born again" biker and a carnival roadie whose singular purpose appeared to be ensuring we all knew (and could recite on demand) the specif-ics of his many sexual conquests. To hear him tell it, women love greasy guys that maintain the "Zipper" at small-town fairs. With little personal experience on the matter, it was hard to distinguish the truth from the lies, but he certainly spoke convincingly.

He lasted less than two weeks before he quit in a flourish of profanities. Evidently the lure of sleeping beside the warm glow of a purring generator while fluorescent lights lit up the night sky was too much to resist. He did leave behind his collection of porn, a mostly full jar of Vaseline, duct tape, and instructions that involved a squirrel.

We could basically be lumped into two broad groups. Group A was those of us that had chosen tree planting because we were ambitious and hardworking, and liked the outdoors. Group A was made up primarily of university students desperate to cover tuition and those who had deliberately chosen to make a career in the bush. The rest, who I will politely refer to as

Group B, were unemployable screwups. Pot-smoking hippies, former criminals, those with social disorders who (by choice or otherwise) would never be able to hold down a regular job in society. The bush was the great equalizer and those differences really didn't matter. All that mattered was whether you could do the job. If you could, you had the respect of the crew, and who you were and what you might have done in another place and another time was mostly irrelevant.

Our designated campsite was little more than a short dirt road located off a slightly bigger dirt road, surrounded by stumps and debris, located smack in the middle of nowhere. Think less summer camp and more a place where Bigfoot would go to die.

The site had been selected for its proximity to the cut blocks where we would be working and because, at the end of the unceremonious dirt road, there was a small, muddy pond. The pond was to become the water source for our shower. Despite what you might be thinking, you can get clean with dirty water.

Cliff quickly began distributing orders. We were to leave our personal stuff where it was. The first priority was to construct the camp itself, namely a cook shack, an eating tent, a drying tent, the shower, and two toilets. The trailers that held the necessary materials were opened and we were organized into crews of two or three and assigned specific tasks.

One group located a suitable place to dig two holes over which a plywood base could be positioned and a small, wood-framed outhouse could be assembled. The outhouse, like all of the structures, was a series of wooden studs cut to fit within a puzzle of steel corner brackets that were then nailed together to create a frame over which a specially designed tarp could be placed. Digging the holes was a difficult task as the soil was typically rocky and filled with roots and other impediments. Mind you, digging the holes and assembling the outhouses was certainly much preferred to taking them apart. Poop smells. A months worth of poop collected from the bowels of roughly fifty people smells even worse.

Assembling the cook shack was the biggest task. The shack was sixteen feet by thirty-two feet and required the assembly of a plywood floor upon which multiple stoves, sinks, cupboards, and counters were assembled together with generators, lights, freezers, and fridges. Once complete, the cooks needed to be able to prepare enough delicious and nutritious food to keep several dozen people well fed and happy. Good food was essential to good morale, and it all started with the careful construction of a functional cook shack capable of keeping us dry and warm in the weeks to follow.

The eating tent and drying tent were quite straightforward—two-by-four studs fitted together over the driest spot we could find. Given neither of these tents had a floor, it was important to ensure good drainage, so we were careful to avoid any natural low spots, and drainage ditches were dug along the exterior perimeter to direct the rainfall away. The drying tent was also outfitted with a wood-burning stove, and a supply of dry wood was collected and stored within for use as needed. Rain was a certainty and snow was common; we had to have a place to dry our wet clothes and, at times, our sleeping bags. After a day of heavy rain, sleet, or snow, the drying tent would be filled with soaked and dirty pants, socks, and boots hanging from the ropes strung between the rafters. The smell was reminiscent of a pack of wet dogs.

The showers followed the same basic construction but were always built a couple feet off the ground to give gravity the opportunity to carry the grey water away to the nearby pit we had dug for that purpose. The shower structure included a small open changing area separated by a tarp from three evenly spaced showerheads. There was no opportunity for modesty. Generally speaking, women only showered with women and men only showered with men, but not always. Every camp had a certain personality that dictated the social norms that were adhered to. The camps I typically found myself in had more "bible school" types than "free-loving hippie" types, so my opportunity for voyeurism was sadly limited. I did have the pleasure of working in a camp with an "open shower" policy for a few weeks at one point in my tree-planting career, but given my (justified) fear that I would be unable to conceal my excitement, I chose to pass on the opportunity. It is one of my biggest regrets.

The showers consisted of a pump drawing water out of whatever water source was available, which was, if we were lucky, a river or lake and, if we weren't, a muddy pond or, in some instances, stagnant puddles. The water was then fed through a flash propane heater that delivered warm, high-pressure water. It generally worked very well and, much like food, was critical to ensuring good morale and maintaining some sense of normalcy.

Showering quickly became a significant social event in camp life. We would literally be caked with mud and sweat at the end of a hard day, and it was incredibility refreshing to shower. No one ever showered alone. You would always find a friend or two to visit with while you went through the ritual of bathing together. Sounds creepy, I know, but it really was not.

With the camp assembled and functioning, Cliff now gave us permission to set up our own tents and get our personal affairs in order. A two-hundred-foot dirt logging road does not give you many options, so Vern and I settled on a spot we determined to be about halfway between the cook tent and the showers. Why have to walk too far for either?

We quickly cleared an area of sticks and rocks and set up our tents before draping large tarps over top. The tarps were important to ensure we kept dry and also created a large porch off the front of the tent in which we could store dirty clothes and other

155

personal items. I neatly arranged my cot and sleeping bag and set out my flashlight and minimal personal items. It was sparse and simple, but cozy enough.

With everything arranged, we wandered toward the smell of food wafting from the cook shack where we found a simple supper of spaghetti and raw vegetables waiting for us.

We filled our plates to overflowing and found a place at a table where we ate in relative silence among strangers who we hoped would become friends. I carefully studied each man in the room, wondering what had brought them all here and whether they had the intangible qualities that would allow them to succeed. I did not know it at the time, but of the twenty-four of us quietly eating our food, only four of us would still remain in six short weeks.

With little to say and no energy to say it, we soon found our way to our beds as the sun began to set and the cold mountain air started to creep into camp. I had bought a sleeping bag, which boldly claimed to be sufficient for temperatures as low as minus four degrees Celsius. Unfortunately, I had not understood that it was going to get a lot colder than minus four and being "rated" for a specific temperature was simply a loose promise that you had a reasonable chance of surviving the night if the stated threshold was achieved. It was most certainly not an assurance that you would actually be warm and comfortable.

I had a miserable first night and woke shivering uncontrollably in the darkness within an hour of nodding off. My nose was cold and numb, and my body was chilled to the core and desperate for warmth. I burrowed deeper into my sleeping bag and clutched my shivering frame, reluctant to set aside all comfort and fumble about in my cold tent in search of additional clothing. It became apparent that my strategy was having little impact, and I began to seriously consider that I may perish before having ever planted a tree.

Chastising myself for my weakness, I threw back my covers and lunged for my clothes. I stumbled in the dark to find as many shirts as I could and pulled them each on, cursing to myself as the cold clothes drew what little warmth my skin contained and swallowed it up. The rest of the night was more of the same, momentarily drifting off before waking disorientated and cold, so while I was exhausted, the morning light brought a sense of relief.

I crawled from my tent and made my way toward the warm glow of the kitchen and the purring generator. The air was cold and damp and the ground was painted white with frost that crunched beneath my feet. Entering the cook tent brought immediate comfort; the small space was warm and filled with the smell of bacon and eggs, pancakes, and coffee. I filled my plate and took a cup of coffee. I hated coffee, but seeing how nobody knew that, and given that clasping the hot mug would warm my stiff fingers, I resolved to give coffee a chance.

The routine was always the same in every camp: wake; eat a hot breakfast; make lunch from a table filled with bread, meats, cheeses, sweets, and fruit; fill your water jug; and make your way to a vehicle. Our waking time was ultimately determined by the distance to the cut block. If we were lucky enough to be within thirty minutes of our destination, we would typically wake about seven o'clock, be driving by seven thirty, and work from eight to five thirty. However, the hours could vary considerably. My worst experience was a four o'clock wake-up, followed by a three-hour drive, which lead to a fifteen-minute helicopter ride before arriving at the block. We would plant until seven in the evening and then make our way home for an eleven o'clock supper before falling into bed exhausted. Fortunately, we only had to endure that schedule for three days, but given I was a foreman at the time and responsible to drive the full six hours while others slept, it was a miserable stint.

157

I was a strange mix of nervousness and excitement as we drove to the block on that first day. I remember admiring the beauty of the natural landscape and then being taken aback at the contrast of the cut block with its severed stumps and haphazard piles of discarded slash. The land was rough and unwanted and lay naked before us, revealing all its imperfections.

We exited the trucks and gathered around the supervisor in our shiny boots and unblemished bags. The supervisor was a diminutive, middle-aged woman, whose leathery skin and matted hair spoke of a life in the sun and wind. She seemed impatient and slightly agitated at the sight of so many rookies standing nervously before her. She already knew what we were about to learn: tree planting is gruelling work and many that attempt the job fail spectacularly.

With no time for pleasantries, she explained the fundamentals of the job itself and the specific requirements of the contract. Trees were to be placed in appropriate soil with the correct balance of organics and situated within the middle of a "screef" the size of a dinner plate. The plug must be fully covered, but the tree could not be too deep, too shallow, or leaning. We could not have J-roots, or cut roots, or compacted roots. Air pockets were *verboten*, as were holes that filled with water or rocks, or that did not close at all. But the most confusing of the seemingly endless requirements was the need for proper density. At any given time and any given location, a checker was supposed to be able to throw a plot and count eight perfect trees within the confines of the circle. Not seven, not nine, but eight. Oh, and if there were "naturals" (meaning trees of the same species that we were planting), then those were to be counted within the plot.

"Wondering what a plot is?" she asked rhetorically as she thrust her shovel into the ground and reached for a simple rope with a loop that she placed over the handle. "A plot is a circle with a four-metre radius," she replied, answering her own question as she pulled the cord tight and began to walk in a deliberate circle, holding the end of the cord while the other end remained anchored by her shovel.

"See this rope? This is a plot cord. You are all going to make one. It must be EXACTLY four metres in length. You will have it with you at all times, and you WILL throw at least three plots each and every hour to make sure you are doing it right. And if you are NOT doing it right, you are going to dig up every tree you have planted and you are going to replant them."

"DO YOU UNDERSTAND?" she yelled.

We nodded in compliance, but it was a lie. We had been overwhelmed within the first minute of the lesson. I for one most definitely did not understand. How in the hell were we supposed to perfect the endless list of requirements while somehow miraculously placing the correct number of trees into the ground and do it all fast enough that we could actually make money? I could see by the panic in the faces around me that many were having second thoughts.

"Alright, let's get at it then," she ordered.

We were then shuffled back into the trucks and dropped in groups of two with a box of trees at one-hundred-metre intervals along the rutted logging road.

I was disappointed Cliff only left one box, as I was confident I would have that planted in no time and did not want to be sitting around waiting for more trees. I had come tree planting to make money—a lot of money—and that was not going to happen if I was parked on my ass waiting for trees.

Despite my concerns, I bit my tongue and unloaded my bags, shovel, lunch, water, and daypack, and Cliff gave us final directions.

"Alright, see that hill?" he asked.

"Yup," I nodded.

"Plant straight toward the middle of the crest; run a flagging line as you go. Vern, you go to the right; Mark, you to the left. This road snakes back at approximately ninety degrees around the corner, and I will start someone heading perpendicular to you. When you hit their line, stop and turn around and fill the space until you have trees on all sides. Got it?"

We nodded, another lie. All I saw was a mess of rocks, stumps, and discarded branches strewn upon an ugly and unforgiving landscape. But I thought I would figure it out soon enough and was anxious to start making some serious money, so I was relieved when Cliff jumped back into the truck and sped away.

Vern was equally concerned that Cliff had greatly underestimated our work ethic by leaving us only a single box of trees, so we agreed to split the box equally, two hundred trees each. We stuffed the three pouches that made up our planting bags, took a quick swig of water, grabbed our shovels, and began.

Each tree was to be placed within the middle of a screef the size of a large dinner plate, meaning we had to make a small clearing, removing all branches, grasses, and other debris until a patch of rich soil was revealed. If the terrain was forgiving, a few kicks with our heavy, steeled-toed rubber boots would suffice, but often several aggressive swipes of the blade of our shovels were required to cut through matted roots and to clear rocks and twigs before revealing a suitable spot. Bent over with one hand on the T-grip and another positioned low on the shaft for power, I would cut at the ground, throwing heaps of debris between my legs. Then I would thrust the blade into the centre of the screef while driving the tool home with a fluid kick. Simultaneously I would be pushing the handle forward to open the earth and then sharply back while my left hand carefully retrieved a tree from my bag and deposited it into the resulting hole. I would then kick the void closed as I stepped forward and repeat the process hundreds if not thousands of times daily.

Dozens of times each day, my shovel would catch a root as I swiped at the ground or strike a rock as I plunged my shovel into the earth. In each case, the shock would reverberate up my arm and through my back. I recall planting one particularly harsh block in which the constant jarring caused my wrist and forearms to swell and bruise to the point where I lost my grip and was forced to tape my hand with hockey tape each morning, fashioning a makeshift cast that allowed me to hold the shovel so that I might continue working.

Lorin Werle, me, and Christine Harris, tree planting in Northern British Columbia

As the weeks and months passed, the exercise became automatic and instinctual, but on that first day, it was truly overwhelming. We stumbled along like lost children with no confidence. Trying to decide where each tree should be placed and how much distance to leave between each seedling was baffling. The task would be challenging enough in your backyard garden.

When you add the relentless buzz and bites of the mosquitoes and flies and the severity of the landscape, which never permitted more than a few unobstructed steps, it was quickly evident that the stories of the brutality of the job were not embellished legend but firmly rooted in truth. These revelations did not particularly frighten me, but they were madly frustrating as I was anxious to succeed and I had not anticipated that I might have to wait patiently for experience to equip me with the skills needed to achieve my goals.

By day's end, I was tired and sore and had not even planted enough trees to cover my camp costs of $23.50 for the food and shelter provided by Tawa. I was not alone in my defeat; in fact, most people had done considerably worse. We were a dejected and humbled bunch at the supper table that evening.

We sat in groups after our meal, comparing our blisters and seeking guidance from the veterans as to the tricks of success. What I came to learn over six years of tree planting and hundreds of thousands of trees planted is that there is no trick. The solution was simply to work hard, to push through pain, and to move forward relentlessly and with tenacity.

The first people quit on the third day. The reasons were always the same: "It's too hard." "It's impossible to make money." "This is not what I signed up for." They were right; on the third day it was all of that and more. Had they stayed, they would have discovered it was in fact doable, but the sting of current failure was more powerful than a promise of future success, so they quit, and kept on quitting, until there were only four of us left by season's end.

It never got easy. It was and always will be among the most gruelling and unforgiving jobs available, but I came to love it. I loved it, in part, because I was successful at it and made a considerable amount of money (it took five years of working in law before I began to equal my tree planting per diem), but mostly I loved it for the friends I made and the experiences we shared. There were unique and amazing moments that could not be replicated anywhere else. Those snapshots in time when I would stop, perched high upon the mountain, and stare down into the vast valley below and marvel at the rawness and isolation of the scene. Or when we would gather and push the largest boulders we could dislodge down the mountainside while we howled with delight as they crashed to the bottom. Or those nights when we huddled with our tribe around the warmth of a blazing fire under an endless sky while the rest of the world was safely tucked in their comfortable beds, not knowing what they were missing.

Dad combining, 1999

CHAPTER 20
THE LAST HARVEST

My dad was diagnosed with cancer on August 24, 2007. I remember the tearful telephone call from my mom and the way her voice cracked, revealing the diagnosis before her words could.

Facing the possibility of losing someone you love is a terrible reality. Your mind races as you try to make sense of it all. There is fear of the disease, fear of what you know of it and what you do not. Fear of the inevitable path that lies ahead and the knowledge that you are helpless to change it. Fear of the hospital visits to come, of watching someone you love endure poking and prodding, pain and discomfort. Fear of uncomfortable silences, of saying the wrong thing, of being too weak or too strong. Fear of the outcome and the potential for great loss. Fear of unfathomable emptiness and a void that could never be filled. Fear that, should the disease win, your children may be too young to remember his contagious laugh, his strong hands, or the sound of his voice.

In the days and weeks that followed, the collective energy of our family was focused on ensuring everything that could be done was done to understand the extent of the disease and that treatment was immediate and aggressive. And of course, through it all, the needs of the farm remained.

It was a miserable fall. Dreary, cold, and wet. Several times each day, I would check the weather forecast from my desk, hoping for the possibility of a stretch of hot, dry weather for the week-end. Whenever the odds seemed better than not, I would throw a few things in a bag on Friday and make the six-hour drive from Edmonton back home to Shellbrook. As the city faded behind me, my mind would race with the responsibilities of my work left behind and the memories of harvests that had come before. The hours dragged in the lonely, unproductive isolation of the car as I raced to my destination.

There was something therapeutic yet undeniably painful about those trips home. I was able to come to terms with Dad's illness and the impact it was having and would continue to have on our family, but I was also forced to accept that this harvest was almost certainly our last and that a way of life, something that had had a tremendous influence on who I was as a person, something that I was passionate about and that had given me so much, would soon end.

I questioned the choices I had made in my life and wondered whether they had all been right, whether they had truly been the best for my family and me. Had I given enough? Had I worked as hard as I could have or as I should have? What if I had stayed on the farm? Could I have made it work? Could I have accomplished as much or more with my life? What would the farm have become if I had dedicated my energy and passion into making it all it could be? Would I be happier, have less stress, laugh more? Was I fulfilled now? Were the long hours and the unrelenting grind of the city, of my profession, of my life, worth it? Had I denied my children the opportunity to experience so many unique and wonderful things that only the farm could have given them?

I had always thought I would return. The plan had, after all, never been to leave for good but simply to experience some of what else life had to offer and, more importantly, to make enough money to sufficiently fund the capital acquisitions that would have been necessary to transition the farm into a viable business in the new millennium. When I decided to pursue a career in law, it was not because I wanted to be a lawyer, far from it. I have always wanted to be a farmer and I still do. I saw the law as nothing more than a means to an end. A supposedly lucrative profession that would provide the disposable income necessary to fund the land and machinery I was going to need. I certainly never contemplated that the farm might be sold, that someone else would actually take possession of something that had such deep, personal meaning to me. I had always assumed I would be successful and that that success would grant me the freedom to buy the farm regardless of whether or not I actually returned to operate it. It was humbling and profoundly disappointing to realize that would not be possible, that Dad could no longer manage on his own and that the farm would have to be sold.

Strangely enough, this conclusion also brought a certain sense of guilty relief, especially in light of the fact that the decision had been made for me and was outside of my control.

As much as I had enjoyed the countless hours I had spent throughout the years walking fencelines and driving machinery, that commitment had, at times, been a sacrifice for me. I did miss out on certain things others enjoyed and took for granted, especially as a young adult. A hot Friday night in September during my university days was not spent drinking cold beer on a patio. Instead it was on the combine or the swather or spent hauling bales. Most Fridays, for each of my seven years of university and for years after as a young professional until moving to Edmonton, I would make the journey home each and every weekend during the harvest to help, returning late Sunday to collapse into bed only to wake up and head to class or work early the next morning. The cycle was the same in the spring with seeding and throughout the year whenever an extra hand was needed.

I didn't do it for the money; I was never paid for my help. I didn't do it on orders, as I was never once told I had to come home. My parents would not have uttered a single word had I said I could not make the trip because of a date or a party, or for no reason at all. There were occasions when I did not go. But that was rare. I almost always went. I went because I felt it was the right thing to do, because I felt a sense of duty and obligation, because I loved my parents, because I was a hard worker and liked the sense of accomplishment a weekend of hard work gave me, because they needed my help, because I could contribute in a meaningful way, but mostly because the farm was a part of me and I knew no other way.

And so, I once again found myself making the journey. I bounced along the highway as fast as the road would allow, while trying to ignore the constant buzz of my Blackberry. The trip was longer and the commitment greater, but so was the need.

The transition to the farm has always been easy for me. Even after ten years as a lawyer, I still didn't feel particularly comfortable in a suit and much preferred coveralls and boots. I have no issue with getting a little dirty. I am not scared of getting a callous. Trudging through the bush, checking fences, shovelling grain, repairing machinery—it all feels very natural to me. I enjoy it. It is an honest, no-nonsense kind of work, and there is something very tangible and fulfilling about working with your hands and being outside all day. It feels healthy. It is good for the soul. And while my involvement in the farm had been declining in the years leading up to Dad's illness, nothing had been forgotten. I still remembered the details of the machinery, that the old John Deere tractor needed a shot of ether and that the hydraulics took a while to warm up. I knew to watch for the continual motion of the ribbon Dad tied around the return elevator shaft on the combine. Flip, flip, flip, as it whipped around, confirming everything you couldn't see was turning as well. I know the smell of a burnt belt and when a bearing has gone; I can hear the subtle difference of a loose chain and can tell whether the swath is dry by the feel of the straw in my hands and the crispness of a single kernel between my teeth. These are lessons that you do not forget.

Each trip I would arrive late, step out of the car, and walk toward the house, looking upward in hopes of seeing the stars and the promise of a hot and sunny day to follow. The night sky had always been one of my favourite things about the harvest. It could be magnificent. At the end of the day, after shutting down the combine for the night, I used to stand alone in the darkness and stare up into the heavens. The stars were infinite and the northern lights could send a chill up your spine as they danced effortlessly across the horizon, filling the sky with pulsating reds, yellows, and purples. It was as if God had a gigantic neon snake by the tail and was playfully pulling it along while it struggled to break his grip. As I stood in awe, I would marvel at the great mystery of it all and enjoy the serenity of the moment.

That fall, unfortunately, there were few stars to be seen as low, dark clouds lumbered by in a seemingly endless march. With no sun to dry the swaths, I spent much of the first morning home breaking apart a beaver dam that had been constructed upstream from our pasture. I smiled to myself as I contemplated the contrast twenty-four hours could bring. The previous morning I had been sitting behind a desk of files, negotiating a multi-million-dollar real estate transaction, and now I found myself wrestling mud-drenched branches from putrid water as I worked to undo the efforts of a family of beavers.

The dam was causing flooding in the large slough that made up much of our pasture. The cattle would not wade into standing water to eat the slough hay that was an important part of their diet, so the water had to be drained. So I splashed about, yanking and pulling on logs and shovelling big scoops of heavy, thick mud until the water began to rush out and drain away. It was the second time I had destroyed the dam that summer, and Dad had done it several times himself as well, as beavers are incredibly resourceful and determined animals, always returning to fix the damage done. They were less determined than their human counterparts, however, as each time they rebuilt the dam it was smaller and weaker than the time before. They would eventually move on, realizing the futility of it all. That is one of the things I have always loved about the farm. Each morning brought with it a certain sense of adventure and unpredictability. You never really knew what you might find yourself doing from one day to the next.

As the water gurgled behind me, I walked up out of the small valley along the well-travelled cattle trails, ducking the poplar branches and spider webs until I found myself at the northernmost edge of our land, staring out into the open pasture and the barns and granaries of the farmyard in the distance. The cows were there. Some were grazing on the short grass of fall, others were sitting contently, chewing their cud while their plump calves perked their ears and bravely took a few curious steps toward me. I stood there as the last golden leaves of fall fluttered around me, and I wondered if I would ever again find a reason to stand in that spot. I instinctively scanned the herd, checking the cows for engorged udders, which would suggest their calf was not eating. I watched them walk as I moved toward them, looking for signs of a limp, listened to their breathing, checked their eyes for infection, and examined how they held their heads and any other sign that they were not well as I mingled among them. Then I stood silently and enjoyed their company as they did their best to ignore me, before making my way toward home, hoping the afternoon would bring sun and a chance to combine.

The sun never did shine on that trip home. There was no shortage of work, however, as Dad and I walked miles of fenceline together over the next few days, ensuring the cattle would remain contained once Dad was laid up following his impending surgery.

Fencing is a gruelling job. It is not too bad when you are fortunate enough to have a fence that runs along an open field, but when it snakes its way through sloughs and thick bush it becomes downright miserable as you are forced to march along beside it, carrying fencing pliers and staples, wire, an axe, a post hole digger and as many posts as your shoulders can bear, looking for breaks in the wire, rotten posts, and fallen trees.

I fenced with Dad countless times in my life. Even as a young child, I would trudge along beside him, carrying a hammer or dragging a single post as mosquitoes nipped at my flesh. If we needed more staples or another post, I would run through the trees, jumping over fallen logs and dodging branches on my way back to the truck to retrieve the required supplies before racing back, doing my best to ensure Dad did not have to wait too long. Sometimes, if we were going to be gone for long, we would pack a lunch wrapped in wax paper and placed in an old four-litre ice-cream pail together with some water or lemonade in a pickle jar wrapped in newspaper and haul it along in a packsack on my back. I can remember sitting alone with my dad in the shade of a big old poplar tree as the leaves rustled playfully above us, eating cucumber sandwiches with dirty hands, knowing that there was nothing else I would rather be doing.

As we walked the familiar fencelines once more, I handed Dad tools and supplies as needed and took the time to enjoy the process and breathe in the crisp fall air. Many of the trees on our path were old and tired as years of cattle grazing at their roots and scratching off their bark had taken its toll. They leaned awkwardly, gaunt and frail and gnarled; many had fallen and littered the pasture. Years earlier we would have taken the time to pile and burn the limbs. It didn't seem to matter so much anymore, and we were content to simply confirm the fence was secure and that the cattle would remain contained.

The primary income of the farm had always been generated by cattle. Typically, eighty to one hundred calves were born each spring and often finished completely before being shipped to slaughter. That meant we were feeding as many as 250 head of cattle on the yard at times as the cows, together with calves at foot and a majority of the yearlings, would overlap for a few months each spring. That many cattle consume a lot of feed, and hauling bales was always a big part of the summer and fall as we worked to bring enough feed and bedding into the yard to see us through the cold winter months to follow. Hundreds of large round bales, some consisting of alfalfa and brome grass, others of sweet clover, green feed, and slough hay, together with a hundred more of straw, had to be collected and hauled home to be stacked in neat, orderly rows. Thousands more of the smaller, compact, square bales made almost exclusively of straw also had to be retrieved from the fields and brought into the yard before the first snow.

Hauling bales had always been a favourite job of mine. Collecting the larger round bales was relatively straightforward. Driving a tractor hitched to a long, flat, metal wagon stretching for thirty feet or more that was broad enough to accept two bales across its width, I would snake through the fields, stopping within ten or fifteen feet of each bale. Dad would then roar in with a loader tractor, scoop up the unsuspecting bale, and place it on the wagon. Depending on the wagon, we would haul eleven or fourteen bales per trip, each bale weighing in at well over a thousand pounds. An equal number of bales would be placed on each side of the wagon, with one less making up a top row perched equally on both of the bales below. I was always careful to count how many bales had been placed on each side as; following the placement of the initial bale at the front of the wagon, it was difficult to see over it to determine exactly how many more were needed to complete the row.

Communication was through a series of hand motions and head nods as it was hopeless to yell over the roaring engines. Dad would point or nod at a bale or a series of bales and I would then manoeuvre the tractor and wagon into position, making it possible to add the bale to the load. Round and round the field we would race, filling the wagon. Mice would often scurry out from beneath the bales as they were raised from the ground. As a youngster I viewed mice as potential pets, but that perspective changed by adolescence. Jumping from the tractor with a burst of adrenaline, I would run through the field, chasing after them as they darted their way through the maze of stubble trying desperately to find another bale to take refuge beneath before meeting the sole of my boot. If hawks or seagulls were circling overhead, I could remain seated and watch in silent admiration as they swooped down and saved me the effort.

Following placement of the last bale, Dad would jump from the loader tractor, jog over, and climb into the seat of the tractor for the ride home. I would slide to the fender and sit perpendicular to Dad, locking one foot into the bracket securing the seat to the Massey Ferguson 285 to ensure my safety as Dad opened up the throttle and lurched the tractor and its load toward home. As I got bigger, the sitting on the fender become awkward for my size so I would stand on the hitch behind the seat and hold on to the fender with one outstretched arm in the shadow of the load as the little tractor belched out smoke and diesel while it screamed down the road and the asphalt blurred beneath me.

Once home, I would guide Dad into place as he attempted to perfectly line up the load with the one previously deposited. When satisfied the load was properly placed, Dad would tip the wagon and engage the orbit motor. The bales would then be dragged from their perch as the thick metal cables attached to a steel barricade situated at the front of the wagon were coaxed to the back, taking the load with them. Dad was always careful to maintain the correct amount of tension on the load so as ensure the bales would not roll off the wagon clumsily and disrupt the perfect symmetry he was hoping to achieve. I can remember secretly hoping the bales would tumble recklessly as that would result in wonderful mazes, caves, and forts perfect for exploring and playing in on lazy Sunday afternoons.

Dealing with square bales was much more difficult. Each bale was approximately three feet long and twenty inches wide, and weighed in at anywhere from fifteen to one hundred pounds, depending on the crop in question and the moisture content of the straw. The cattle consumed four to five thousand of the small rectangular bales yearly.

An automatic stooker, dragged behind the square baler on a

combination of skids and wheels, would snatch each bale from the back of the baler as it was ejected and ferry it along a short conveyer to the top of the machine where it would be dropped through a mechanism that looked much like partially opened saloon doors. As each bale pushed the doors back, the machine would count one, dropping the first bale lengthwise into the centre where it was held in place by two collapsing metal plates. Two bales were dropped on one side of the centre bale and three more on the other to create a small golden pyramid of straw. When the sixth bale passed through the trap doors above, a trigger was sprung and the stooker would lurch back and deposit its load onto the stubble before springing back into place with a loud clank and starting the process all over again.

I can still hear the sounds of baling. The continuous roar of the tractor engine against a background of clattering steel pickup teeth eagerly grabbing and throwing the crackling yellow straw up into the baler where it was immediately swept into the bowels of the machine and greeted by a plunger, which cut and pounded the straw back into a square chamber with a rhythmic *thump, thump, thump* as it cycled back and forth, compressing the straw and creating the bale. *Roar, clatter, crackle, swish, thump, thump, thump, roar, clatter, crackle, swish, thump, thump, thump* in an endless symphony.

Transporting the bales home was a considerable task as each one had to be hand stacked onto the wagon. Dad would shovel up the stooks with a loader and gently place them on the wagon, careful not to break the twine holding the compacted stalks together. Two men on the wagon would then hurriedly work in unison to stack the bales as quickly and tightly as possible before another stook was deposited.

There was an art to stacking square bales. The objective was to stack each load eleven bales high, being the highest point possible without clipping the power line that ran across the road from our house to a small machine shed located on the yard. That resulted in more than three hundred bales per load. Each bale had to be deliberately and forcefully placed in a specific and consistent pattern, or the load may not hold and could collapse either in transport or while being unloaded. So we followed the same arrangement load after load, year after year, stacking the bales together in accordance with a deliberate design.

With each layer the base would shrink marginally, as the pattern was designed to create inward gravitational force. By the time the final bales were inserted, there was little room to manoeuvre as we balanced precariously high above the ground. When the final bale was slid into place, the men stacking would carefully step into the bucket of the outstretched loader and be lowered to the ground to admire their workmanship and double-check the tires before making the trip home.

When I left home to attend university, Dad coincidently acquired an automatic picker that eliminated the need to manually stack square bales. So, like many of the traditional jobs of the farm of my youth, stacking bales by hand was no longer necessary. Instead, a picker operated by a single person sitting on a tractor was simply pulled around the field, collecting and stacking the bales into perfectly uniform rows.

I spent several days hauling round bales that fall. The familiar smells and noises had not changed as we raced around the field collecting the harvest. It felt just as good to stand back and admire the symmetry of a perfect load, just as nice to give a half wave to neighbours as we tore down the road while asphalt blurred beneath us and exhaust billowed up into the grey sky.

As it does each harvest, the sun finally broke through the clouds, granting us the opportunity to combine. Our combine was a 1984 Massey Ferguson 852 pull type bought at auction many years earlier for $8,500 and hitched behind a 1983 Case

2390. It was in good shape for its age, having always been shedded and well cared for. Its paint was still bright red and it decals remained intact.

In its time, it was the biggest pull type combine manufactured by Massey Ferguson. It could easily eat its way through fifty acres a day, perhaps more, depending on the size of the swath. By comparison, the first combine I had ever operated on the farm, at the age of twelve, was a Massey Ferguson 410 open-air self-propelled combine that had been manufactured in the late sixties. Compared to that, the 852 was a monstrous machine with significantly more capacity. I remember driving the 410 in my early teens in the searing heat of the fall as dust billowed off the parched swath ten feet in front of me. The engine, located approximately two feet from the seat, generated significant heat at full throttle. The combination of the sun, the screaming engine, and the thick, dry dust made for a dirty, sweaty experience as I followed swaths around the fields.

The grain tank on the 410 held about ninety bushels and was located an arm's length behind the seat. It ran the full width of the machine and hung over the sides of the chassis like saddle-bags on a horse. Dad had built a tank extension out of two-by-six wooden planks, which expanded the capacity to approximately 110 bushels, less than half of what a modern combine would hold. If you stood on the seat and stretched backwards, you could push the grain around the tank, filling the corners in an attempt to squeeze in a few extra bushels before finding a waiting grain truck.

Its paint was dull and faded and the seat had long since worn away. A foam cushion covered in plastic and wrapped in tape was placed on the exposed wood base to provide some protection from the vibrations and bumps. The steering wheel, big and strong and moulded from hard plastic, was situated immediately in front of the seat parallel to the floor. One hand would hold the wheel while the other alternated between the levers, which controlled ground speed and the pickup.

It ran beautifully for such an old machine. Dad spent days each fall checking every chain, belt, pulley, and sprocket. Once confident the machine was ready for the task at hand, Dad would idle the engine on low, engage the thresher, and slowly walk around the machine, listening intently for any squeak, rattle, or vibration that would hint something had been missed. Following inspection, we would take the combine to the field and make the final necessary adjustments, ensuring the cylinder was the proper distance from the concaves and running at the proper speed to properly thresh the grain from the straw. If the gap was too tight, the machine would lose capacity, crack the kernels, and plug too easily. If too wide, the kernels would not shell from the head. It was a delicate balancing act.

The same exercise was followed with the sieves. Dad would fiddle with the angle of each grouping and the wind speed of the fan below in an attempt to coax the grain to fall between the rows of aluminum fingers to be whisked away to the tank while simultaneously encouraging the straw and chaff to continue bouncing on out the back of the combine.

When the tinkering was complete, we would pull into a swath and I would drive at a crawl while Dad walked along beside at the back of the combine, holding a grain shovel in an outstretched arm, catching samples of chaff as it was spit out the machine. If an unacceptable amount of grain was found among the chaff, all the settings would be checked and rechecked, repeating the process until Dad was confident we were getting all we could expect out of the old machine.

I always waited impatiently for the process to be completed, eager to get started with the real work. Then, with a wave of his hand and a subtle grin, Dad would give the all clear and I would excitedly increase the ground speed and force the combine to eat the swath before it as fast as possible while simultaneously being careful not to let it plug. When the swath was too heavy, the cylinder would let out a booming *whump* and belts would scream and smoke as the engine laboured to power through the straw. When careful attention was paid to the ever-changing size of the swath, the ground speed, and the location of the pickup table, plugging could generally be avoided. There were times, however, when, despite our best efforts, the machine would suddenly lurch awkwardly as it lost power and the deep *thump* of the cylinder stopping abruptly could be heard echoing across the field.

A long, thick metal bar was carried on the combine for just such occasions. Angry and frustrated, I would jump from the seat and stand on the pickup table above the feeder chain that conveyed the straw from the pickup into the cylinder. After opening the trapdoor that gave access to the cylinder, I would begin coaxing the combine to regurgitate the straw by forcing the feeder chain and cylinder backwards with the metal bar. If the plug was relatively minor, that exercise would work and little time would be lost. More often than not, the machine was crammed so tightly that, despite pulling on the bar with every ounce of strength I could muster, it would not budge. It was then necessary to cut and pull as much of the firmly packed straw as possible out of the throat of the combine in hopes of relieving enough tension that the machine could be forced to spit out the oversized bite.

The process could take hours. Lying on my back in the dust and the heat as my outstretched arms ached, I would work feverishly, cutting and tearing away small handfuls of straw from the inside of the machine where it had been jammed by the full force of the engine. Bit by bit the straw would be removed until the cylinder could be forced to turn and the balance of the straw was finally muscled out the front of the combine.

I hated plugging the combine. Not so much because of the gruelling work fixing the problem necessitated, but because of the sense of frustration and embarrassment it brought. I wanted so badly to do a good job. I never wanted anything to jeopardize my opportunity to contribute to the farm. I feared that Dad might conclude managing the machine was beyond me; I was, after all, only twelve years old when I started driving it. So when I did plug it—which was not that often—I worked as hard and as quickly as I could, trying desperately to fix the problem before Dad discovered me and was forced to leave the grain truck or baler he was operating to help.

◉ ◉ ◉

We started on a crop of barley that fall. The swath was modest. The unrelenting heat of the summer sun combined with insufficient rain had stunted the stalks and shrivelled the heads. When the rains finally came in late September, they were much too late and simply aggravated the problem, pounding the swaths flat into the stubble, making them difficult to pick up, and encouraging spouting as the grain sat pressed against the wet earth.

Then came the geese. Hundreds would descend on the crop, swooping in uninvited and unwelcome, gorging themselves with little concern to the damage being done. With each passing year, geese were becoming a bigger and bigger problem, due largely to a lack of hunters, which had traditionally managed the population and kept the pests at bay. Fewer hunters equalled more geese, and more geese meant less profit as the birds were capable of tremendous damage, easily reducing the value of a crop by twenty percent or more when considering the amount of grain consumed and the fact that goose scat among the grain would result in limited markets for sale, typically reducing the grain to cattle feed.

When I pulled into the diminished swath, the machine easily handled the load. Unfortunately, the swath had been packed so tightly into the stubble by the unrelenting rain and geese that it was difficult to retrieve and the pickup struggled to do its job, forcing me to keep the speed low as I manoeuvred around the field. I did my best to push the combine, coaxing the machine to do its job while Dad alternated between baling the straw and hauling the grain to a waiting bin when a truck was filled. It was the same scene that we had played out countless times before as we worked desperately to cover as many acres as possible before Dad's looming surgery.

Farming is a combination of ingredients and variables. You can control the ingredients, deciding what crop to seed, how much fertilizer, herbicide, and pesticide to use. But the rest, the biggest parts of the puzzle, are determined by a combination of unpredictable variables completely outside of your control. Despite the most carefully drawn plans, and no matter how hard you might work, no farmer controls the rain, the temperature, the date of the first frost, the wind, the price, hail, snow, and the countless other things that determine whether money will be made or lost. Each year is a gamble; you simply hope that overall, in the larger scheme of things, you win more often than you lose. To succeed in farming, you have to be an optimist. You have to believe that next year is going to be the one, the year when the rains come on cue and the crops flourish under the perfect sun. Notwithstanding the trucks filling slowly and the quality of the grain being poor, we concentrated on the positives: we were finally moving forward, the task before us was shrinking, and the next field, we hoped, would be better.

It was better. Considerably so. But the weather refused to abate for long and the sky soon filled with clouds and the air turned damp and cold. With two hundred acres left to combine,

I headed back to the city, wondering if the rest would wait for spring.

It didn't have to. A few weeks later, in late October, I received an excited call from my mother. The harvest was done. All of it. Every bushel was in a bin. The relief in her voice was palpable.

Our neighbours had left their own fields and pulled into ours. With four large, modern combines between them, they made short work of our outstanding crops. That help, at that time, when it was so badly needed, meant the world to my family and me. I wish I had been there to see it. It would have been a beautiful sight to see those big machines rip through the swaths while men scrambled to haul the grain and Dad directed traffic. I wish I had been there to see them pluck up that last swath.

I loved that last swath. I always wanted to be the one on the combine when it was picked up. There was something deeply satisfying about knowing a job well done was complete. That another season had passed, that the pressure was off and the snow could come should it please. We would come in from the field, shake off the dust, and sit around the table with bloodshot eyes, eating and drinking and reliving it all with smiles and laughter. It felt so good. We were all so happy, proud of our collective accomplishment.

I will miss that last swath and the satisfaction of watching the last few feet disappear into the combine. I will miss harvest suppers in the field and hot plates wrapped in towels. Sitting on the tailgate of a half-ton truck surrounded by family eating potatoes with gravy and home-raised beef from a plate on my dusty lap while the oranges and reds of the endless prairie horizon disappeared into the evening. I will miss the smell of diesel and dust and the way the stubble crackled under my feet in the afternoon heat. I will miss the night sky and the endless stars, watching flickering lights in distant fields, the sense of solitude, the sense of togetherness. I will miss the roar of engines, the swoosh of grain pouring into an eager truck in an endless, blurring stream. I will miss the late-night trips home, weary and covered in dust, at the wheel of an old grain truck as it laboured down narrow dirt roads, creaking under the strain of its load as the moonlight cast shadows in the trees.

Greg Spencer (long-time hired man), Dad, Albert Balla,
Kristin, and me at the auction, 2008

CHAPTER 21
THE AUCTION

The farm auction was held on Monday, May 5, 2008. It was the perfect day for an auction, pleasant and warm but not so nice so as to convince people there was something better to do, and with the fields still wet from a late spring snowstorm, there was no reason for attendees to feel guilty about skipping a day on the tractor.

Dad had spent months sifting through a lifetime of tools and equipment, organizing his life's work into neat piles and rows. Wrenches, pliers, saws, screwdrivers, shovels, nails, and bolts were all sorted and bundled into lots. Every extension cord, oilcan, and spare part was gathered up and added to a pile. Each shelf, drawer, and bucket was emptied of its treasures. The granaries were searched and the rafters of the barns scoured. Old wagons and machinery that had long since been laid to rest and forgotten were awakened from their resting spots under the shade of the sprawling maple trees, which lined the north boundary of the yard, and reluctantly manoeuvred into place. The tractors and implements were meticulously cleaned and polished and carefully and deliberately lined up in two long, neat rows. By the morning of the auction, it all sat naked and exposed to the prying eyes of neighbours and strangers to be picked over and assessed while we stood among the crowd and reminisced quietly to ourselves.

The 1974 Massey Ferguson 1085, the one and only new tractor Dad ever bought in over fifty years of farming stood in line, as did the first tractor I had driven in the fields and the 1949 Fargo Grandpa had bought decades earlier. It is a strange feeling to see the memories of your youth lined up for sale to the highest bidder. As I walked among the equipment, I took the time to climb into the seat of the tractors, grip the wheel, and imagine one final drive while I reminisced about the many happy hours I had spent bouncing along through the dusty fields on those very seats. As a child, before I was old enough to operate the machinery, I had spent afternoons doing the same thing in the summer sun, yearning for the day I could drive the tractors with my dad. I climbed into the cabs of the trucks and savoured the familiar smell of grain and dust, and hopped up and peered into the empty truck boxes one last time. It was an emotional day. Our family had worked the land and called the farm home for sixty-two years. Sixty-two years of work and sweat, of clearing the land of trees to expose the soil, of constructing the barns and corrals, of raising cattle and harvesting crops, of building a home, of raising a family and making a life. It's hard to see that all come to an end in a single afternoon, to watch it all be shuttled off the yard, piece by piece.

I never thought it would come to that. Growing up, I did not even consider it a possibility. I loved the farm and everything about it. I remember putting in a new stretch of fence in the field just west of the farmyard with Dad when I was twelve. We worked from sunup to sundown for the better part of three days that summer to get the job done. First we yanked every fencing staple from the posts, saving each one before carefully rolling hundreds of feet of rusty, brittle wire. All the old, rotten posts were pulled and piled and then we picked a new line and started fresh, pounding in several hundred posts in a perfectly straight line before stretching out and nailing on four strands of shiny new wire.

The fence looked beautiful when we were done: strong, sturdy, and perfectly straight. As we stood there admiring our handiwork, I asked Dad how long a fence like that might last.

"Should be good for thirty years with upkeep," he responded.

I remember doing the math in my head and smiling to myself, concluding that the next time the fence needed replacement I would do it with my own son. That was how my mind worked. I was the only son, so I would take the farm on when Dad was ready to retire. It was that simple. I dreamed about the time when my day would come, when the reins would pass to me and I would be responsible to continue on the work my dad and his father before him had started. I never imagined anything else for my life.

But life is unpredictable and takes you in directions that you cannot always anticipate. When I finished high school, the farm was simply not big enough to generate income sufficient to sustain two families, and we did not have the money to buy more land and larger equipment to farm it. I was ambitious and a good student, so I went to university with the plan to work hard, make money, and come back. My plan never changed. As the years passed and I found a life and career off the farm, I had come to accept that it was unlikely I would ever return to the farm full time, but I certainly thought I would buy it, that the land would stay in the family. When Dad got sick, all the timelines were accelerated; we no longer had the luxury of waiting to see how it would all turn out. Dad could no longer manage the farm on his own and I was not at a point where I could afford to buy it, so there was little choice in the matter.

Surprisingly, Mom and Dad were probably the least upset about the sale. They certainly shed their share of tears in the weeks and days leading up to the sale but, for them especially, there was simply more to be happy about than sad. Dad had seemingly beaten cancer and was healthy. The endless work and responsibility that had followed them for the entirety of their adult lives would soon end. Never again would Dad be up at three in the morning, wrestling with some miserable, ungrateful cow struggling to deliver her calf while Mom stood at his side, directing the beam of a flashlight. Never again would Dad have to work late into the night on the seat of a combine or fumble with tools in the winter cold, fixing a tractor. Finally, for the first time in their lives, the weather would become nothing more than a topic for casual conversation or perhaps a minor annoyance. An early frost, excessive heat, drought, or hail no longer cost them tens of thousands of dollars and sleepless nights. With the farm sold, Mom and Dad could head to the lake on a sunny Sunday afternoon and enjoy an ice cream by the beach without worrying about cattle getting into their crops or those of their neighbours. Life on a family farm is a wonderful experience, but it is hard, unrelenting work. Everyone deserves a break from that at some point. Mom and Dad certainly did, and after they came to grips with the initial disappointment of selling, they began to look forward to the slower pace of retirement.

So we all found ourselves together, early on that grey Monday morning, making final preparations as people began to wander and collect around machinery. All of my dad's five siblings were there, as were their children. So was my mom's only brother. All the hired men who had helped Dad with the farm work over the years came, as did the neighbours. Each shook our hands in the comforting way you do when greeting a family mourning a loss, and then they slowly wandered around the yard, letting their own memories fill their faces with a smile.

Kendall, me, Luke, and Kristin at the auction, 2008

The farm had meant a lot of things to a lot of different people in many different ways. For Dad's brother and sisters, who had called the farm home for many years themselves, the sale served as a reminder of their own mortality and of how many years had passed. It was especially hard for my aunts, as the auction, combined with the fact we had buried their mother the year before, must have left them feeling like they had lost a big part of their family and the last strong connection to the memories of their childhood.

If Grandma had still been with us, I am not sure Dad could have gone through with the sale. Grandma was a saver; to her everything had value and was to be kept and cherished, especially something as precious as the farm and the tools and equipment the family had used for years to make their living from the land. It would have been devastating for her to see it all go, to watch the handlers walk among the crowd, waving an old rusty rake or a cream can high above their head while the auctioneer searched for a bid of a dollar on something that was so valuable to her. The cavalier way tools and trinkets were hastily bundled together and shuffled off in quick succession would have broken her heart. Grandma would not have understood the reasons that made selling the right choice, nor would she have understood the necessity of the process.

For my sisters and me, the sale marked the end of something that had always been a big part of our identity. We were farm kids, and we were proud of that fact. I never missed the opportunity to tell people I was a small-town farm boy from Northern Saskatchewan. In my mind, it suggested we were an honest, hardworking, no-nonsense kind of folks. We were people that could be trusted, that wouldn't snivel and whine at the slightest hint of discomfort, but would simply put our heads down and stoically push through the obstacles life placed in our path. We did what we said and said what we did. There was no mystery to us, no bull; you knew what you were getting each and every time. Low-maintenance, tough, and dependable. With the farm sold, it felt like I had lost a little bit of my credibility, like I would have to add a caveat anytime I mentioned I was from a farm.

The sale also marked the end of many family traditions we had grown up with and enjoyed. Our childhood had been simple. There were no trips to Europe, or anywhere else for that matter. No weeks at science camp, expensive new clothes, or closets full of toys that never got played with. Instead we would run wild through the bales, playing tag or hide-and-go-seek, build forts in the trees, trap gophers, and capture frogs. We would ride our bikes for miles down the road without worry or concern, raft in sloughs, pick wildflowers, skip rocks, wrestle with the dogs in the grass, and run barefoot in a freshly tilled field relishing the sensation of the cool, moist earth against our bare skin, but all of these things came only after the work was done.

Our time before and after school was not filled with television or video games; we were busy with work and responsibilities. Even in the dead of winter, I would waddle outside in the dark before the sun was up, bundled from head to toe to gather eggs, feed the chickens, and carry water to the 4-H calves before going to school. I remember coming into the house and shedding snow pants frozen stiff from the water splashed against my legs as I struggled with the heavy pails. I loved it. I always felt needed, always felt important, always felt like every single day had meaning and purpose and value. I spent hours with my dad every day, working. I got to know him and I learned from him, not just how to fix a tractor or mend a fence, but how to be patient, how to take a breath and think before acting, how a kind word is almost always better than a harsh one, how to say you are sorry and take responsibility for your actions, and the value of hard work and the true meaning of strength. Perhaps the hardest part of watching the farm sell was knowing that I was losing the opportunity to have those same experiences with my own children.

My son, Luke, is like me in many ways. He had just turned seven the month before the sale, and watching him tear around the farm that weekend yelping and laughing and smiling filled my heart with joy. He found a little old red bike that Mom had salvaged from a garage sale. It seemed he forgot how to walk, and he rode it everywhere. It was no more than eight degrees Celsius, but skinny little Luke stripped off his jacket and shirt and furiously ripped around the yard half naked with a big stupid grin on his face, yelling nonsense as his little legs pumped the pedals for all he was worth. It's just what I would have done. Up and down the yard he rode, searching for any sort of hill to maximize his speed as he weaved in and out of people and machinery while his cousins chased along behind him.

Luke on the red bike, May 2008

The bike was finally abandoned momentarily when Luke and his cousins Drew and Kurt discovered the round bales. Those wild boys ran and chased each other around and on top of the bales, giggling and laughing in the crisp, fresh air until they were overcome with exhaustion. It was deeply satisfying to watch them all enjoy the same games I played as a child and to see it bring them the same joy. It was equally hard to realize that they would not have the opportunity to play such games again.

Much of the weekend was about just that, about experiencing things for one final time. One last walk through the barns, one last peek into the sheds or ride on the tractor. So on Sunday afternoon following church, we packed up hot dogs, buns, and all the usual accompaniments and made our way to the clearing located in the middle of the home section for a family wiener roast. It is the most beautiful place on the farm. Entering from an adjacent field, you make your way along a grass trail lined with poplar and spruce trees, down a hill into a five-acre clearing where pockets of bluebells, yellow buffalo beans, and orange prairie lilies strike a contrast against the thick, green grass in the summer sun. In the most northwesterly corner, there is a break in the trees opening up into a smaller, secluded clearing nestled on top of a knoll. There is a small pond at the bottom of a gulch off the south point with cattails hugging the edges and frogs and ducks splashing about. It is a peaceful, picturesque, charming place that is filled with happy memories of picnics and campouts.

As we sat eating and reminiscing, the children ran among the familiar trees playing the games children do. Soon the boys began to instinctively construct a fort from broken branches to fend off imagined attacks from the uninterested girls. They huddled behind their barricade with sticks in hand, congratulating themselves on their clever plan and daring the girls to approach. We lingered until long after the fire had gone out, waiting for the children to tire before making our way back home.

That night, my brothers-in-law, Adam and Glen, and I took our sons night hunting for barn swallows. The boys were incredibly excited, notwithstanding the fact they had no idea what it was they would be doing. They did understood it involved guns and flashlights and that the girls would not be coming, so they were convinced it would be fantastic. As a child, I would often take my pellet gun and a flashlight and head off into the barns after dark in the summertime to search the barns and granaries for the small birds perched among the rafters. I would scour every crevice of each rafter with the beam of my flashlight, hunting for an unsuspecting bird. When one was found I would direct the light into its eyes, blinding it while I took aim with my pellet gun. A quick, twangy pop would be followed by a small, muffled thud and a poof of feathers as the swallow tipped and fell to the ground. I would shoot two dozen or more in a night and pile them up neatly for the cats to enjoy.

So we walked out into the yard as the sun was setting and made our way to the barns. I quickly taught the boys how to direct the light, what to watch for, and the importance of gun safety, but the barns were empty. For whatever reason, there were no birds that night. So we kept walking past the barns, looking for targets to substitute for the missing birds. As we walked, we startled two deer that had been grazing on the short spring grass. They bolted past us, bouncing into the air with their tails held high flashing white against the darkness. We stopped and watched them run and in the silence of the moment heard coyotes howling in the distance. I couldn't help but smile.

I had always loved the haunting sound of coyotes. My earliest memory of an encounter with a coyote was when I was eight years old. We had two female exchange students staying with us that summer, one from Ontario and another from the Philippines, eighteen and sixteen respectively. I remember working in the garden early one evening with Lisa, the Canadian, and hearing a chorus of coyotes beginning to howl. It sounded as if an entire pack was standing at the eastern edge of the yard. Lisa was intrigued and wanted a closer look so I grabbed my pellet gun and the two of us began to jog in the direction of the howling.

As we approached the far end of the yard looking out into the pasture, the silhouette of a large coyote emerged from the trees and confidently trotted to the top of the dugout hill. The animal was still a hundred metres away, but I clearly remember the feel of my heart in my throat as I watched that wild animal standing on a hill, staring back at me across the distance. I was terrified and mystified all at the same time but, at eight years old, had no intention of taking another step in the direction of the animal. Unable to convince Lisa the time to turn around had come, I handed her my pellet gun and she continued on alone in an attempt to see how close she could get. I perched myself on the top rail of the nearby fence as darkness settled in around us and watched her jog quietly toward the coyote while slouching coyly in an attempt to avoid detection. The coyote played along for a few minutes but, before Lisa could get close enough to pose any real threat, it turned and disappeared back into the forest.

The boys felt we were plenty close enough to the coyotes that night as well, so we took turns shooting at old cans until the sun completely disappeared and the boys grew cold.

I was up early the next morning, anxious for the day to begin. By seven thirty the big, shiny red trucks of the auctioneer began to file into the yard. A truck pulling an office for bidders to register and pay arrived, another pulling bathrooms and one more hauling a concession stand—all made their way into the yard.

They were incredibly efficient and organized, with a half dozen men or more bustling about attending to the many details. Soon the office was opened, the bathrooms were functional, and the smell of hamburgers was filling the air.

As advertised, at ten o'clock sharp while people continued to file in, the auctioneer grabbed the microphone and began to sell. He started with an assortment of tools and trinkets Dad had neatly organized and arranged on the bale wagon. Pails of nails, a bundle of shovels, a handful of rope, wrenches and pliers, it all sold in rapid succession. There was a buyer for almost everything and, if the item in question could not draw a bid, then something more desirable was added to the lot in order to attract a bidder. In the end it all went, every last screw.

Each buyer was identified by a number. "Number 263 gets the wrenches; I'll tell ya boys, that was a bargain, we're giving stuff away here today boys, you just try to find yourself some wrenches looking that good at the store for half that price, it ain't right boys," the auctioneer would taunt the crowd.

Meanwhile, number 263 would be shuttled off in an ATV to his truck in the adjacent field/parking lot to drop off his newfound treasure and then hurry back in time to bid on the upcoming items.

Auctions are fun to watch. A good auctioneer is incredibly charming and has a way of making every bidder feel like a genius for raising their hand. The only time you will ever regret a purchase at an auction is the next morning because, at the moment of sale, you are made to feel as if you practically stole the object in question from the fools around you who clearly do not have your same eye for value. An auctioneer plays on your pride, asking you to imagine how good you will look pulling into the field with that big, beautiful tractor, to think about how fast the crop will come off with a combine of the calibre sitting before you here today.

In auction talk, "old" equals "antique" and if it was bought within the last ten years it is "new" or "barely used." Every engine and each implement is in unbelievable shape, field-ready and able to the get the job done. If it's broken then it's nothing that you cannot get going in a couple minutes at home. Every single item has dozens of uses and represents boundless opportunities. A long-handled shovel with a circular scoop, which we had only ever used to scoop chunks of ice from a freshly cut hole in the dugout when watering cattle in the winter, was described by the auctioneer as having multiple applications, including not only scooping ice but also dirt from the bottom of a deep post hole where a normal shovel could never reach. I had not thought of that, and that shovel had never seen the bottom of a hole in the time it spent on our farm, but I remember thinking he was right, it would be great for that.

Uncle Manfred, top left, Uncle Terry, top right, Aunt Iris, Delbert, Dad, Uncle Terry, Aunt Elsbeth, and Uncle Manfred, bottom, at the auction, 2008

At one o'clock that afternoon, following a short break, they began to auction the large machinery. Before starting, the auctioneer gave a short history of our family, telling the quiet crowd how Grandpa had come from Germany as a young man and spent the rest of his life making a living from the land. He spoke of my dad continuing the work of his father and building up all that we saw around us. How my aunts and uncles and my sisters and I were all raised on the farm, that we were all here to show support for my parents on this momentous day. It was short and simple and I found myself getting choked up. And then it began, the 1946 Mercury one ton was the first to sell, followed by the 1949 Fargo, neither of which had been started in years. Those trucks were old and decrepit and of little use to anyone except a dedicated soul determined to restore them, but it was hard to see them sell nevertheless as they had been a part of the farm since near the beginning. Down the first row and up the second, they progressed through it all one implement at a time. Delbert quickly took over, jumping into each truck and tractor to start it up and do the obligatory ten-foot drive forward and backwards, confirming all was in order. I was glad he did; for some reason, it did not feel right to do it myself. I had been to many auctions over the years, but this one felt unfamiliar and somewhat surreal. I found myself standing alone at the edge of the crowd, making occasional small talk with friends and acquaintances or answering questions about the machinery, but mostly I just watched quietly, uncertain how to feel or what to do, yet very aware of what was happening and its relevance and wanting some space to absorb it all.

Me, Luke, and my nephew Drew, the morning of the auction

In a little over two hours it was over. The yard began to buzz with activity as successful bidders settled up in the office and scurried about the yard, collecting their winnings. I ran around with Dad, helping the new owners hook up to the implements or load their loot while people began to stream by with tractors, trucks, and equipment that hours earlier had been ours. It was a blur of activity and emotions. As the last of the machinery was making its way off the yard, I stripped off my coveralls for one final time and gave my parents a hug, told them I loved them, and then loaded my family into our car and began the six-hour drive home, dreading the responsibilities of work that awaited me the next morning.

As we pulled out of the yard, the emotions of the day overtook me and I began to cry. I cried for many reasons. Partly because I knew I would never again sit in a tractor seat and watch the golden stubble turn black as a disc rolled the earth and filled the air with the musty smell of fresh soil. Because never again would I sit perfectly still among fresh straw in the warm spring sun, waiting for the approach of a curious calf while the melting snow dripped from the roof of a nearby barn. I cried because I would never again be at the wheel of a combine as the last swath made its way into the machine, because I would never again feel the deep satisfaction of a bumper crop. I cried because our family traditions now had to change, and because my children had only got a small taste of all the farm had to offer. I cried because I knew I could never get it back; it was gone forever and there would be no second chance. But mostly I cried because I felt a twinge of regret. The only job I had ever truly loved was that of a farmer. Nothing else had given me that same sense of accomplishment, that same deep gratification and content-ment. I wondered again if my choices in life had been right. If I should have chosen a different path.

Cousins Brent and Grant Grams, Anita O'Dwyer with Erin, Heather, Aunt Inga,
Mom, and Aunt Ruth at the auction, 2008

Ultimately I believe that everything happens for a reason, that to a certain degree, fate will chart our course and we simply need to be receptive to the opportunities that life presents. It is true, I think, that we make a choice to be happy, to be successful and fulfilled. Quite simply, life is exactly what we believe it to be. So I chose to believe that my life has been, is, and will be amazing, fulfilling, and rewarding. That is not to say I am not disappointed that my future no longer includes the farm. I am, but the lessons the farm has taught me and the memories it has given are mine, and selling the farm will never change that. I have been blessed in countless ways, and the privilege of enjoying many years immersed in a family farm is but one of those blessings. I desperately wish there had been another plausible option, but there wasn't. So I still get up each day and thank God for all he has given, for a wife who loves me, for happy, healthy children, for the ability to provide for my family, and for the mysteries and challenges that the day will bring. I have found my peace.

Mom and Dad at the last farm picnic, 2008

Glen, Rachel, Erin, Kristin, me, Kurt, Kendall, Drew, Anna, Mom, Luke,
Dad, Heather, Colleen, and Adam, spring of 2008

CHAPTER 22
LESSONS FROM
THE LAND

As a child, I envisioned my future with precise clarity. I would become a farmer like my father and his father before him. The possibility of doing anything else with my life did not even cross my mind.

About the time of my fourteenth birthday, I began to become aware of the fact that my parents were working extremely hard simply to survive and keep farm debt manageable. Depressed global markets, unpredictable weather, and the ever-increasing cost of production continued to plague the agricultural industry. I heard the grumblings of our neighbours and friends as they sat drinking coffee around our kitchen table. I saw the worry in their darkened eyes and the way they shook their heads and wrung their blistered hands. I knew that my parents could not afford to simply give the farm to me and that, despite the fact our farm was diversified and relatively secure, there was no way two families could survive off the income it generated.

Out of necessity, my focus shifted. I would attend university, convinced that a higher education would correlate to a higher income, which in turn could be channelled into the farm. Post-secondary education was simply to be a means to an end. If all went well, I told myself, I would return to the farm within ten years with a solid financial base. Those ten years quickly passed, and despite two university degrees, stable employment, and careful financial management, I was never able to achieve my goal.

I have been away from the farm for many years now and, sadly, all the land, machinery, and animals have long since been sold, but the farm still continues to be an integral part of my identity. Of all of the experiences I have had in my life, nothing has affected me more profoundly or had a greater influence on determining my character and values. For good or for bad, the farm is the single most defining element in my life. Everything I came to believe and understand originated with the farm. That is not to say the story ends there. Each encounter and every other experience in my life is built upon that foundation, but the core of who I am is unquestionable.

The farm taught me the value of family, that more can be achieved by working together than by struggling alone. From the time we were old enough to walk, my sisters and I were expected to contribute in any way we could. Whether it be planting the garden or weaning the calves, we tackled the job together. Each of us was delegated a task and expected to complete the job properly and without complaint as we worked beside our parents to achieve the goals set for us. I came to understand the security of being able to lean on others and the responsibility of having others rely on you.

The farm taught me the importance of hard work and that most of life's obstacles can be overcome by sweat and perseverance. I can remember how it felt to pull into a wheat field filled with thousands of square bales scattered across the landscape. Each one had to be picked, stacked by hand, and delivered home. It was a daunting task that could only have been achieved by committing to dirty, physical work. Not once did we stop to complain about the scope of the job before us or bicker about who would do what or that there was too much to do. We would simply, and without hesitation, pick that first bale and then continue picking and stacking as hard and as fast as we could until the field was clean. That is how we approached every job. We were taught to take pride in a job well done and to enjoy the process. Work was never something to be feared on the farm, it was what we did and we were fiercely proud of that fact. We were taught that when there was work to be done you did it, you did it well, and you did it without complaint. It was that simple.

The farm taught me respect for the earth and the importance of treating our planet well.

Farms are schools of natural history, ecology, soils, seasons, wildlife, animal husbandry, and land use. As a student of our farm, I know, for example, which hills will erode in wind and rain, and which conservation methods to use to best defend against such erosion. I understand how it is fruitless to seed the saline portions of the west quarter to canola if a dry spring is forecast because, without the rains to leach out the salts, the crop will fail. To me, each field has a different smell, a different texture, and a different story. I remember fall rye so tall it touched the brim of my father's cap, and crops so light you could barely see the swath. I came to understand how our actions would influence each of these outcomes.

I know where the best berry patches are and where the geese nest. I could find a tiger lily, a crocus, or a buffalo bean because I know where each of these flowers grow. I have walked every fenceline and skipped rocks in every slough. My sisters and I have spent hours scouring around the old homestead sites that once occupied each quarter, picking up little pieces of glass with awe and marvelling at the history and adventure of it all. There is no other profession more integrally connected to the earth than farming, and my years on the land convinced me that we must nurture and care for the planet to ensure it will in turn provide not only for us, but for the generations to come.

The farm taught me humility and optimism. I remember quiet, solemn suppers, watching the crops shrivel and die in the blistering summer sun, and the sense of profound helplessness that accompanied the heat, but I also remember the giddy, childish joy that filled me when the much-needed rains finally came. Farmers are constantly reminded that there are forces much greater than themselves determining their destiny. Despite the best-laid plans, meticulous execution, and relentless hard work, crop failure was never more than a hailstorm or early frost away. Living with that reality helped foster a certain modesty and encouraged optimism, as hope was often all we had. Many times I heard our neighbours joke that we lived in "next year country." That is how we viewed our world and how we coped when nature refused to cooperate. The farm taught me that worry for the sake of worrying never accomplishes anything, so why bother. Work hard, do all you can to determine the outcome you desire, but beyond that, let it be and accept what fate has in store, because doing anything else will make you crazy and gets you no closer to your goal.

Perhaps most importantly, the farm showed me who I was. It gave me a sense of purpose and belonging that ensured I had the strength and confidence to handle the challenges I have faced in my life. That is not to say I haven't experienced failure or that I have not made bad choices, because I certainly have. But when you know who you are and are comfortable with that, warts and all, you will find yourself much better equipped to live the best life possible. I was never particularly concerned about my inadequacies because I knew that I was a hard worker and that I was a valuable part of our farm. I understood that I was needed, that I was important to my family, and that each and every day I could contribute in a meaningful and tangible way. That knowledge gave me an immense sense of comfort, confidence, peace, and fulfillment, and as a result I never had to go looking for a feeling of worth or contentment in other places. We were given responsibility so we became responsible; we were expected to work hard so we became hard workers; we were ignored if we complained so we became hardy and determined. Children learn what they live and a family farm is a demanding teacher.

Hauling round bales with Adam Marshall, my brother-in-law

All these experiences have bound me to the land. The farm has become a part of my identity and soul, and will always be such, regardless of the fact that it is no longer ours. The traditional family farm is much more than just a vocation; it is a distinct cultural experience that is quickly becoming extinct as economies of scale force farmers to expand and develop a more sophisticated approach to the business of farming.

Fifty years ago, it would have been a given that the farm remained within the family unit, as a child almost always stayed at home and continued the family's farming operation. That is not the reality of contemporary agriculture.

The changing face of agriculture is a reflection of two realities. Firstly, it is only possible to be financially viable if you have a large farm. The capital costs of modern equipment cannot be justified if you only crop a few hundred acres. When spending millions of dollars on tractors and combines, you need thousands of acres on which to run them. There is simply no other equation that works, and the inability to access the tremendous amounts of capital needed creates a barrier that quickly excludes many.

The second factor is directly connected to the first. When you create a massive farm with a multi-million-dollar annual budget, you change the dynamics of the business. The farm loses the cozy and inviting "mom and pop" feel as it becomes, and is run as, a serious operation. It is no longer a son on the combine while dad hauls grain and mom delivers supper to the field. Dad is now stuck at a computer, fretting over futures contracts; mom is coordinating the delivery of catered meals to a whole crew of seasonal workers; and the son is probably at hockey practice because lack of integration resulted in lack of interest.

Business is ultimately consumer driven and, given the primary message delivered to the farmer is "give it to me cheap," farmers have no choice but to comply. So, farms will continue to get bigger and more automated in the continual quest for efficiency and profit. Nothing will pass our lips that has not been genetically modified and doused in chemicals, and children will leave the farm, leaving the land to be gobbled up by corporations.

There is a social consequence when these farmers leave the land. That is not to say an outsider would not, or could not, properly farm the land. They may be excellent stewards and learn to cherish the land, but the relationship would never be quite the same. The connection that exists when the fields were broken by our forefathers, when all of our memories are centred on the existence and health of the land, becomes lost when the land is seen as nothing more than a resource to be exploited for gain.

There are no viable alternatives, however, as the family farm of my youth is no longer economically feasible. So farms and machinery will keep on growing as agriculture continues to become more mechanized and sophisticated. That is not to say change is something to fear—it is not—but it is important that we remember the lessons of the past and keep in mind that family and farming are better together than apart.

So, for me, I accept the fact that, like everything else in life, the face of agriculture will change and evolve and that for the most part the family farm of my youth will be experienced by very few in the years ahead. I am thankful for the experiences I enjoyed and for the memories that I hold. I will forever smile at the sight of fields of golden wheat waving gently in the breeze and will always love the musty smell of damp soil. Once a farmer, always a farmer.

Dad and me

ACKNOWLEDGEMENTS

The genesis of this book arose from an essay written in Law School for which I was directed to draw from my personal experiences in agriculture. My Professor was kind enough to encourage me to finish the story, so I did, chipping away at it for the next twenty-three years when time permitted and I was feeling particularly nostalgic.

For me, the story of the farm is the story of my family, and with that in mind I would like to thank:

My sisters, Heather, Colleen and Erin for our shared adventures.

My Mom, for her unconditional love and support (and for keeping me well fed!).

My children, Luke and Kendall, for giving me reason to laugh each and every day.

My wife Kristin, for being both the one I wanted and the one I needed.

And to my Dad, for giving me a childhood in which "chores" were the best part of my day.

My Dad lost his battle with cancer on July 30, 2016 and never had a chance to see this book. He would have liked it, especially the pictures.

Printed in Canada